The Snyff Taker's Ephemeris

Volume

Nine

© 2013, Lucien Publishing.

THE SNUFF TAKER'S EPHEMERIS is published sporadically by Lucien Publishing, Fayetteville NC. Volume Nine, Summer 2013. Cost: 10.99/single volume; 43.96/per year. Address: PO Box 287, Spring Lake, NC 28390. www.STephemeris.com.

Advertising and distribution/bulk purchase queries: distribution@STephemeris.com.

(Our ads are cheap. Don't be afraid to ask!)

ISBN-10:

0985478152

ISBN-13:

978-0-9854781-5-5

On The Cover

At one time New York City's most profitable and well-known snuff shop was S. Scharling & Son's Gambetta Snuff Company.

Unlike most tobacco shops at the time, the Scharlings dispensed with the typical cigar store Indian and in its place went with an 18th century Scottish Tartan holding an empty snuff box.

The shop was located at originally at 110 Division Street (at Orchard) but soon grew so large that it occupied the shops at 110, 111, 112 and 113. This photo was taken by Bernice Abbott in 1936. (The original silver print was auctioned off by Christie's for about $5,000 USD.)

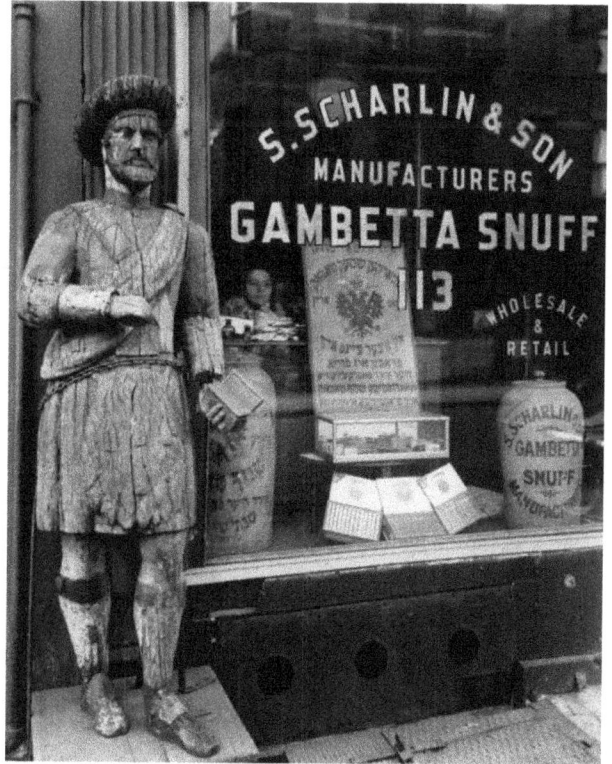

Scharlin Sr. Opened the snuff shop in 1876, with ten gold bars and a quest to make a snuff that would appeal to other Jewish immigrants. Donna Gaines, great great granddaughter of the store's founder, wrote that the Scharlin family came to America from Russia to avoid Jewish persecution in their homeland. Within a few years, they had created a kosher Scotch snuff that they named Gambetta snuff, which was a hugely popular regional brand during the early 1900s. As can be seen in the photo, Gambetta came in two different containers: one with a Hebrew language label and the other with an English language label.

"Her parents," Gaines recalled, "bought leaf tobacco at stands along the Bowery, ground it up, and sold it." Thirty years later the family refused an offer of half a million dollars for their shops. "By the time the depression hit, snuff was passé, and the property was valued at a tenth of its original worth. Today, it's a hair salon in Chinatown."

The Scharlins were well-liked by their community and the younger Scharlin, Sidney, once ran for public office in 1912. He lost (as a Democrat) to the Republican candidate by just a few votes. After the store closed, the family took on different ventures, some profitable and some not. Many mourned the loss of their favorite snuff as the Scharlin and Son Snuff Company closed its doors in the late 1940's.

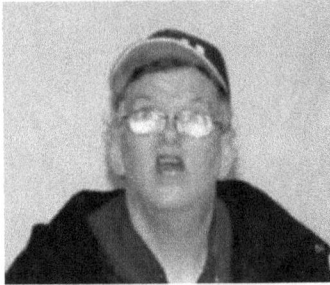

PUBLISHING STAFF

EDITORS

RW Hubbard
President, Publisher

Micah Rimel
Managing Editor

Mick Hellwig
Editor-in-Chief

STAFF WRITERS

Gillian Bromley	Mick Hellwig
Elisha Cozine (Chief Photographer)	RW Hubbard
	Bill Johnson
Seth Desjardins	Nigel McCarren
Jennifer Goldsmith	Micah Rimel
	David Thigpen
Anthony Haddad	James Walter
Simon Handelsman	Larry Waters

Table of Contents

SPECIAL THANKS to Matt Slate, Rick Charles, Marcus Carlsson, Rupini Bergstrom, Steve Abbott, Mike Dean, Falicia Toscano (back cover model), Tara Strongarm, Lilia Luster, Jordyn Ballentine, Go Smokeless.org, Larry Waters, etc.

Letters

DEEP WATERS

I greatly enjoyed Larry Water's article this issue (Volume 8). It's exciting to know that there's an actual bar, like a cigar bar, that is centered around snus. Even though I'm more of a snuff person, I think the idea is grand. I'm now a member of Snuscentral thanks to his article, though I still have yet to taste my first bit of Swedish Snus. Hopefully that will change soon.

L. Frank Hodges,
U.K.

We're glad you like Larry. This magazine wouldn't exist without him.

IN WITH THE OLD

I'm glad to see that the trashy pictures are gone, hopefully for good. This last issue was your best since the early ones. I read it cover to cover and have no problems leaving it laying on my coffee table.

John Cable

Believe it or not, we've had more letters complaining of the lack *of girls last issue. Hopefully we'll try and find a happy medium without offending anyone.*

IN WITH THE REALLY OLD

I'm trying to find the oldest tobacco product

or brand that's still in production today. Any help would be greatly appreciated.

Mark
Nevada

Well Mark, Fribourg and Treyer's snuffs have been around since the early 1700s, though we're not sure what modern blends, if any, are made from those original recipes. The oldest verifiable product would be Swedish Match's Röda Lacket, which has been in continuous production since 1753. It was also the first European snuff to be imported into the United States.

FACT OR FAKED?

The head letter in this latest issue can't be real. Why would a kid be reading a snuff magazine? And why would his father go through the trouble of writing you about it?

Anonymous

Well Mr. A., we solemnly swear that we had nothing to do with that epistle. We're pretty sure it was a gag letter, but we ran it anyway because it was so darn funny.

WHERE DA HO'S AT?

I hope you're not getting rid of the sexy layouts altogether. It brings some nice eye candy, especially the vampire pictorial. Who'd have thought that snuffing could be so hot?

Jae Kopka,
Florida

Opinion about the model layouts have been the hot topic among both our readership and our staff ever since we've introduced those elements to the Ephemeris. The only way we have to gauge the response is through reader feedback, so be sure to keep letters like this coming so we'll know if we're on the right track or not.

Dear STE,

I'm beyond sick and tired of the government telling me what, when and how I can use tobacco or whether or not I can drink alcohol. After reading some of Bill Johnson's articles, I find it amazing that at one time in this country, almost everything was legal, or at least tolerated, concerning drugs and alcohol. What the hell happened? I'm glad you have a voice for your magazine that describes to us young'uns what the good old days were like.

Jamey Cortez

We passed this letter on to Bill, who offered this to say:

"There really is no such thing as the Good Old Days. We use to have to walk out into the snow and use an outhouse in sub-zero temperature. I had a brother that went blind pouring lime dust mixture into that same shithole in order to keep the odor of feces from drifting onto the front porch. And nevermind the black widow spiders lived in there like it was a condominium.

But in terms of human freedom, a fella could do pretty damn near whatever he wanted without someone stepping in and taking it away from him, be it alcohol, tobacco or even things like Morphine or reefer. THOSE were the only good things about the good old days!"

What happened to the pin-ups? At first they pop up out of nowhere and now they're missing. Are you guys (and gals) bi-polar?

Chris Stephenson,
Indiana

As we stated earlier, we're trying to find a happy medium. In all honesty, direct sales have been declining since issue 6, but we're not sure if this is due to reader upset or increased newsstand distribution. That's why we need your feedback more than ever. If we're making a magazine you don't want to read, let us know.

WHICH BARCODE?

When I buy your magazine from my tobacconist, here's what happens. If the clerk scans the UPC code on the back cover, it rings up 10.99. But if they ring up the UPC on the very last page in the back of the book, it rings up 9.99. They always ring up the back cover instead of the inner cover and I feel like I'm getting ripped off for a buck. I know it doesn't sound like much but it still pisses me off.

Judith,
Ohio

Here's the skinny on the two UPC codes. The retailer should be scanning the back cover, the 10.99 price. However...

The inner UPC printed on the last page is a proprietary barcode that serves two functions: it is a printer's identifier code, which most Print on Demand printers use, and it also serves as our direct sales UPC code, which rings up for 9.99, since we sell the book from our website at a 1.00 discount off of cover price.

When a new retailer starts carrying our book, we inform them that they have the choice of moving the book for either 9.99 or 10.99, depending on what they want to sell the book for. Some stores

sell it at full price, others sell it for the discount price. Many stores forego the barcode altogether and sell it at their own set price.

We believe in the free market, and we give retailers the right to sell our magazine for whatever they feel is fair. But we do encourage them to sell the book at a discount if the customer buys snuff, snus or pipe tobacco along with their book. If you email us with this retailer's information, we'll contact him and inform him of his options.

One tobacconist in North Carolina has an unbeatable deal. If you purchase 20.00 worth of smokeless tobacco, you can buy an issue of the STE for 50% off cover price. The retailer isn't losing any money off of the magazine and he's boosting the sale of smokeless tobacco in his shop. For us, it increases the awareness of our magazine among people that normally wouldn't drop 10 or 11 dollars on a book that s/he probably wouldn't buy otherwise. It's a win/win situation for everyone involved, and we hope more stores invent similar promotions in the future.

FULL COLOR?

I love the large, bigass size of the new magazines but I miss the full color of the early issues. Any chance of going back to full color?

Marco

Not any time in the near future. But remember that our digital copies are always full color, and half the price of our printed edition to boot!

See you in 40!

Note From The President

NACS Convention 2013

It's that time of year again. It's the weekend when all of the big names in convenience store products come out to play- the NACS Trade Show.

Formerly known as the National Association of Convenience Stores, **The Association for Convenience & Fuel Retailing** hosts a three-day event once a year where all the retailers, merchandisers, wholesalers and distributors come out to play. Think of it sort of as a comic convention, except that it's not really very fun and there aren't any celebrities there, unless you count such esteemed guests as the guys from **Pawn Stars** or the blonde guy with the mullet from **Lizard Lick Towing**. The Lizard Lick Towing guy was all the rage in the parking lot outside the show, walking around with a phone in his ear and shooing away the peons who asked to take a photograph with him. Never before have I been so star-struck.

The venue itself, The Georgia World Congress Center in Atlanta was huge. It covered three floors and it probably would have taken you about 12 hours to explore the entire convention if you wanted to check out all the booths. Free samples of beef jerky, t-shirts, keychains, pretzels, hotdogs, plastic cups and frisbees were handed out with bacchanalian abandon for all who asked. Beer and energy drinks flowed freely, and even the Sasquatch Jerky bigfoot roamed the floor, touching people inappropriately. Good times.

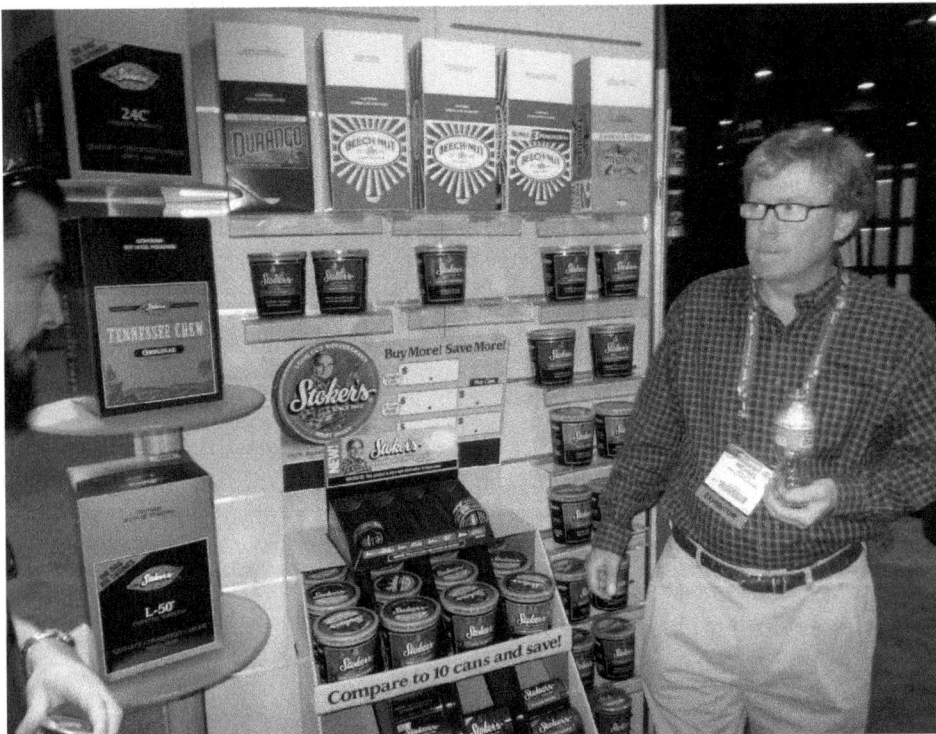

Left: Stoker's Booth.

"We're still focusing on giving the consumer a quality product that gives more bang for the buck."

But we weren't here for the swag. (At least, I wasn't.) I came to check out what was new in the world of tobacco. It's been years since I attended a NACS show, but the presence of tobacco companies was shockingly low compared to what I expected, smokeless tobacco companies even more so. No, the big thing this year was E-Cigs. It seemed like every other booth was an E-cig or liquid vapor manufacturer. The sheer number of such companies tells me that the industry is heading towards a crash not unlike the dot com bust of the late 1990's. I'm guessing that the hundreds of E-cig booths that we witnessed this year will be sheared down to a mere handful by the 2015 show.

The Stoker's booth was a sight for sore eyes. Although they didn't seem to have many new offerings this year, it was good to see that an independent American snuff company seemed to be holding its own in the face of such fierce competition. Stoker's, in addition to their more famous loose-leaf chewing tobacco, has been a constant presence in the lower-to-mid priced moist snuff category for years but has never seemed to be able to bust wide open like the other, more well-known brands. But that didn't seem to stop their enthusiasm at the show, and their spokesman seemed to know quite a bit concerning the manufacture and processing of smokeless tobacco compared to all of the other booth reps we would end up visiting that day.

On the other hand, smokeless tobacco was pitifully represented there by the Big Two. Philip Morris and RJR's smokeless booths were small, unmanned, and had no products on display. To be fair, we showed up late in the day, so maybe they had already packed up to leave. But that still doesn't explain the guy I later bumped into wearing a Copenhagen shirt who said that he worked the booth.

"Where was everything?" I asked. "All I saw was a pamphlet."

"Yep." He kind of smiled sideways at me and walked to the Pom booth. So much for that one.

Thankfully Swedish Match's booth was grandiose without being pretentious. Several pamphlets and flyers explained both their Swedish snus lines as well as their North American moist snuff offerings. Attractive blondes handed out samples to curious onlookers. On hand was the always affable Mike Dean and Steve-o Abbott, describing the new things in store for the General brand (spoiler alert: expect something BIG in the last week of January '14) and the Redman, Longhorn, and Timberwolf snuffs.

The American (round) General tins have been slightly modified into a more streamlined design that sport nifty new catch lids. The American exclusive "General Classic" brand's plastic containers have been completely re-designed into what just may be the coolest snus tin ever invented. All in all, Swedish Match's game plan for next year sounds exciting and progressive.

Clockwise from top: Swedish Match's Mike Dean and Steve Abbott, the new General 2.0 coolers, and the newly redesigned Red Man snuff tins.

Top to bottom:

More Swedish Match porn. The General booth lady; the new Longhorn "tubs" (contains about six cans worth of snuff); and the fresh new Timberwolf and Longhorn single cans.

When launched nationally, the Longhorn tubs just may end up being the best deal in moist snuff on the market. Here in NC, they retail for $4.99 a tub, or roughly 0.83 cents per can. There's even an empty Longhorn container included in the tub in case you don't happen to have one handy.

We next hit up Kretek International's booth. Kretek is one of the fastest growing tobacco distributors in the world, with its eye set firmly on smokeless tobacco. They are the exclusive distributor of v2's snus lines in the US (Thunder, Offroad), GN (Oden's), and Toque's American nasal snuff line, Silver Dollar. Our friend Rick Charles was manning the smokeless side of the booth and was held up repeatedly by tobacco-hungry convention-goers screaming out for samples of the snus and snuff on display. It reminded me of Elvis, circa 1956, being mobbed for his autograph.

Above: *Kretek's Rick Charles. "Move over, Lil' Wayne. I'm the mackest of the mack daddys."*

While representation from the big tobacco companies was underwhelming (or in most cases, non-existent), we were happy to see that there were a few new independent tobacco companies springing up in spite of the new FDA restrictions. Though they all produce mostly cigarettes and roll your own "pipe" tobacco, it does give me hope for the future that more US upstart companies will pick up the torch and attempt to give the public an alternative to the mass-produced crap that lines the shelves today. My only question- why do they all seem to have an Indian/Native-American motif in their name or packaging? I kept waiting to see a pack of "Big Chief Smoke-em-up" Full Flavors laying around somewhere.

Above, left to right: Token Indian posing in front of Smokin Joe's cigarettes and pipe tobacco booth; GoSmokeless.com's Chris Nash standing next to token scrawny blonde booth babe.

Left: Hipster Alert- The Pabst Blue Ribbon booth reveals the brews of yore that are set for a relaunch: Stag, Lone Star, Old Style, National Bohemian, Schlitz, Olympia, Rainier, Primo, Pearl, Colt 45, Black Label, Stroh's *and* Jax. *Where's the* PBR Bock *and the* Champale *at?*

The VIP Afterparty (co-hosted by Swedish Match) was a private party for Really Important People that featured live performances by Beatles cover band The Fab Four and the hottest rapper of 2008, Flo Rida. He lip-synched his fat little heart out and the Fab Four's bizzarro-John urged everyone to do the twist while he sang a chunky-faced version of *Twist and Shout*. The enthusiastic crowd of 50-60 year old white males and their young "secretaries" responded with an overwhelming holler of non-compliance, so STE Managing Editor Micah Rimel and I got in front of 3,000 people and twisted the night away before I slipped in a puddle of gin and fell on my back. Micah tried to save me, but I pulled him down with me and he kneed me in the genitals.

Right: Flo "I Used To Be On TV" Rida.

Below: The Flab Four. They were like a wax museum not come to life.

13

The venue was inside of a really huge aquarium that looked like a James Bond villain's secret lair. I felt bad for the fish on the bottom floor, because the bass vibrations from the live music were throwing them into a frenzy and they were crashing against the glass, completely dazed and unable to maintain a composure due to the catastrophic decibels knocking them off track. I tell ya kid, you haven't truly lived until you've seen a 20-foot shark ram into plexiglass and sink to the bottom of an aquarium floor while old white men scream about spurs and apple bottom jeans.

We left the show around 10:30 and got back to our hotel for a few drinks before turning in for the night.

We'd like to thank Swedish Match for inviting us out to this year's event and for providing us with enough material to write what may possibly be the STE's longest "Note From the President" article ever.

We're looking forward to next year's shindig!

Above:
Television's Ron Shirley of Lizard Lick Towing *calling his manager to inquire as to why Steve Abbott, Chris Nash and Smokeless Aficionado's Rob Jarzombek aren't paying any attention to him.*

Below:
Ephemeris Publisher RW Hubbard waiting for someone to come and ask him for his autograph. He sat in the same spot for twelve hours straight. "They must not recognize me 'cause of the beard," he opined.

EPHEMERA !

Presenting all of the news fit to reprint

UPMC GOES OVERBOARD WITH NEW ANTI-TOBACCO POLICY

The University of Pittsburgh Medical Center recently passed a new set of rules that effect roughly 33% of the health center's staff, along with thousands of patients, visitors, contractors, and interns.

The new policy bans the use of snuff, snus, smoking and even E-cigarettes on campus and prohibits the carrying of such items on a person's being. It is unknown how the hospital plans on enforcing the carry ban. Random pat downs have been suggested, but the overworked and understaffed hospital employees have made it clear that they have no desire to add more workload to their staff.

"Our patients are best cared for, and both patients and visitors have the best experience, when our employees are at their very healthiest and when the workplace is free of tobacco," said Gregory Peaslee, UPMC's chief human resources officer, in a statement.

The hospital, which is running under capacity, has stopped short of not hiring smokers. "We're just getting rid of their work breaks and making sure that they understand the damage that they are doing to their bodies," Peaslee added.

He also stated that he is "open" to the idea of testing medical staff for nicotine in their blood system. Under such a rule, users of harmless smokeless tobacco and E-cigarettes could lose their jobs. The aforementioned staff shortage will probably make this addendum unlikely.

SNUS USE IN PREGNANT WOMEN UNLIKELY TO CAUSE HEALTH PROBLEMS

Compared to cigarette smokers, women who use snus while pregnant are at a much lower risk for health problems than other tobacco users.

Lund University in Sweden conducted a study that spanned the years 2000-2010. They found that on average, a snus using mother-to-be delivered a child that was approximately 1.7 ounces smaller than a child born to a mother that never used snus, a figure that most scientists dismiss as an insignificant percentage.

The authors of the report were quick to warn, however, that "Our findings should not be interpreted as suggesting that the use of snus is a healthier alternative to smoking during pregnancy." But the statistics clearly show that snus is at least 12 times healthier for pregnant mothers than those that smoke cigarettes.

MORE STATISTICALLY INSIGNIFICANT NEWS

The CDC has concluded that E-cig use among high schoolers has doubled since last year. That's 2% of all high schoolers in the USA that have tried an E-cig, compared to last year's 1%.

In his typically over-dramatic fashion, Tobacco Free Kid's president Matt Myer's stated that he was "shocked" and "alarmed" by the figure. He then spotted a cricket on the floor and jumped into the arms of his bodyguard. "Don't let it get me!" Myers cried, as onlookers questioned "what the hell is wrong with that guy?"

CORONA, CALIFORNIA COUPLE SUE VAPCIGS, STORE OWNER AFTER E-CIG BATTERY EXPLODES

RIGHT: XAVIER AND JENNIFER RIES

ORIGINALLY REPORTED BY CBS NEWS, LOS ANGELES

A Corona husband and wife have sued an e-cigarette manufacturer after its rechargeable battery exploded in their vehicle, leaving the woman with second-degree burns.

Jennifer Ries and her husband, Xavier, were on their way to the Los Angeles International Airport for a volunteer trip to South America back in March. Ries said she was charging a VapCigs e-cigarette when an aroma filled the car.

"My husband asked if I had nail polish in the car. I looked around and I saw the battery to the (e-cigarette) dripping. I went to unscrew it and the battery started shooting fire toward me and then exploded and shot the metal pieces onto my lap," she said.

Ries told CBS2's Serene Branson that her cotton dress caught fire. "A blowtorch type of fire and then an explosion," she said.

Xavier said he immediately got the car into the emergency lane. "I let go of (Jennifer) so she could get out, grabbed the coffee that was sitting between us, and threw it on the seat to put (the fire) out," he said.

"I got severe second-degree burns on both the back of my upper thighs and my lower buttocks," said Ries. Ries said she's still visiting doctors at UC Irvine Health Regional Burn Center. "I'm supposed to stay out of the sun for at least two years," she said.

Gregory Bentley is representing the Ries' in a lawsuit against Benham Zolgdahr, the retailer, and Corona-based VapCigs. "When a company, regardless of who it is, puts a product into the marketplace, it should be safe," he said.

Bentley said the bigger issue is that while the e-cigarette industry is growing rapidly, it's not being regulated. "Right now, at least how it stands, the FDA is regulating this whole industry as a tobacco product, so all of the component parts, including the battery, the charger, and so on, are not tested for safety," he said.

"The more this goes on without being regulated, the more it's going to happen," said Ries.

EU SOCIALISTS AND DEMOCRATS USHER IN TOUGHER TOBACCO LEGISLATION

*(Taken from Euractiv, © 2013). All lies, half-truths and misrepresentations have been highlighted in **bold** for your convenience.*

The Parliament's Committee for Environment, Public Health and Food Safety (ENVI) voted Wednesday (10 July) in favor of new rules on tobacco packaging and a ban on slim cigarettes, raising a chorus of complaints from the tobacco industry.

The committee has proposed that a pictorial health warning covering 75% of a cigarette package, front and back, should be mandatory in the EU. The MEPs also want to regulate increasingly popular e-cigarettes and to ban slim cigarettes which are **aimed at young women.**

Irish MEP Nessa Childers from the Socialists and Democrats (S&D) said she was pleased with the result of the vote after **"massive"** industry lobbying against the law. MEPs recently complained that they have been **'bombarded' by the tobacco industry,** which employs over 100 full-time lobbyists in Brussels, and received dozens of e-mails, letters and brochures.

"I am delighted that today we voted against the massive **negative industry lobbying campaign** which tried to delay, block and defeat this legislation," Childers said.

Mike Ridgway, spokesman for seven UK packaging manufacturers, said the ENVI vote represents a victory for the criminal fraternity across Europe and the supporters of the counterfeiter who will find it easier to replicate standardized and simple packaging compared to the specifications currently being used.

"At risk also across Europe are the many thousands of jobs employed by the packaging manufacturers, together with the future investment plans in an industry which has been a barrier over the years to those that desire to market illegal and unregulated product to the young and vulnerable sections of society," Ridgway stated.

Childers, however, argued that tobacco **puts a heavy burden on governments and society as a whole.** Costs include **indirect costs related to workday losses due to morbidity** and **direct costs associated with inpatient and outpatient care.**

"Non-smokers also pay for the costs of smoking, primarily in the form of higher health insurances and medical costs related to second-hand smoke, leading to higher taxes and higher prices for healthcare products and services," the MEP said.

"The focus is to prevent the industry from recruiting new smokers among the young," said British MEP Linda McAvan from the Socialists and Democrats (S&D) who is steering the legislation through Parliament. "The smoking trend is down, **as action by public authorities has reduced the number of smokers over the years**. However, there is a worrying drift: **29% of young people smoke.** The World Health Organization has shown that since 2005, the trend has been **going up amongst young boys and girls in some countries**" she added.

NEW BILL INTRODUCED TO HELP SMALL TOBACCO MANUFACTURERS PROTECT THEIR BUSINESSES FROM THE FEDERAL GOVERNMENT

Alongside twelve bi-partisan co-sponsors, Reps. Bill Posey (R-FL) and Kathy Castor (D-FL) introduced H.R. 792, the ''Traditional State and Local Cigar Manufacturing and Small Business Jobs Preservation Act of 2013". This legislation is a crucial step forward in protecting the premium cigar retail industry from undue regulation by the Food and Drug Administration (FDA) aiming "[t]o amend the Federal Food, Drug, and Cosmetic Act to clarify the [FDA]'s jurisdiction over certain tobacco products, and to protect jobs and small businesses involved in the sale, manufacturing and distribution of traditional and premium cigars".

Though the bill is centered mainly around the cigar industry, it would benefit most small-business smokeless tobacco manufacturers as well.

"The trouble is that Big Tobacco has billions of dollars to fight the feds, who have even more money at their disposal. The little guy hasn't had a fair shake since Obama took office," claimed Marc Rubio.

He urges all supporters to contact their local representatives to draw attention and support to the bill, which could help save thousands of jobs in the US.

EPHEMERA !

S.S.D.C.*

BY
BILL JOHNSON

Is it just me, or is Philip Morris going hog wild since the President signed the **Kennedy / Waxman Family Smoking Prevention and Tobacco Control Act** into law? It seems like every week there's a new damned blend of cigarettes that PM whips up (not to mention their Copenhagen/Skoal flavors- aside from the Copenhagen Southern Blend, it's all pretty much garbage in my mind.)

We have Marlboro Black, Marlboro 72's, Marlboro Special Blends, L&M Red, Yellow, Blue, etc. I get a lot of forwarded mail asking me about this stuff, even though I haven't been a part of the tobacco industry since Fred Flintstone took his first drag off of a Winston. But believe it or not, the production of filtered cigarettes hasn't really changed much since the late 60's, so I'm able to offer up my opinion on some of these new "Crayons."

I call them Crayons, because ever since the new law bans terms like Light, Full Flavored, Mild, etc; all of the new cigarettes are color-coded. Red is for Full Flavored cigarettes. Blue is usually for Lights. White, or weird colors like Sunburn Orange are for Ultra-lights. Green is for menthol, light green for menthol lights, etc. One reason that Philip Morris supported the whole Kennedy-Waxman thing to begin with is that they've always stuck by the color coded method, while other manufacturers preferred to actually create different packaging altogether for their lights and ultra lights. Philip Morris knew that by banning such descriptive pack nomenclature, it would mean that their competitors (mainly RJR) would have to completely redesign their packaging and ultimately confuse vendors and customers in the process. If you're looking for a full flavored cigarette and you can't tell the difference between a regular Camel pack and its milder brethren, eventually you're going to just say "Give me a pack of Marlboro Reds." Or so I've gathered.

So it's time to answer some mail from my letter bag. Mainly the questions have to do with people switching from a Mass-Premium brand like Marlboro or Newport into a sub-premium like Marlboro Blend 27 or Special Blend. I'll explain the cigarette "caste system" in plain terms real quick:

PREMIUM: The most expensive cigarettes on the market. These include Non-filtered versions of Pall Mall, Camel, Lucky Strike along with "old fart" filtered brands like Benson and Hedges, More, and Tareytons.

MASS PREMIUM: These are cheaper than "true" premium cigarettes, and make up almost 80% of total cigarette sales. Popular brands like Marlboro (Reds and Lights) and Newport (Menthol Green)

*SAME STUFF, DIFFERENT CENTURY

dominate the market, and always have. But that market is always fluid, and as public perception of what's "in" waxes and wanes, so do the brands.

For example, we'll look at Tareyton. When Tareyton was introduced, it was one of the few cork-tipped filtered cigarettes, and fetched a premium price. It was more expensive than the Mass Premiums of the time like Camel or Lucky Strike. But as filtered cigarettes became in vogue, Tareyton switched to a new type of charcoal filter and was priced alongside the other Mass Premiums, and it sold very well. After Marlboro was reintroduced in the 1960's, Tareyton could not compete and so the blend was changed (along with the filter, which turned into a conventional cellulose unit) and it became a "generic," priced cheaper than Marlboro or Camels. Finally the consumer base was so small that Tareyton went back to the charcoal filter and became a true "premium" once again, where it has stayed for the last thirty or forty years or so.

Another example is Doral. Once again, Marlboro dominated the filtered cigarette market from the late 60's to the present. Camel Filters just weren't selling, and Winston had peaked in popularity. RJ Reynolds needed a new cigarette that wasn't aimed at any one type of consumer like Marlboro (tough guy cowboy cigarette) or Silva Thins (A mild 100 mm cigarette aimed at the Esquire crowd). [**EDITOR'S NOTE:** *We would now call the guy in the old Silva Thin ads "metrosexual" in the vernacular of today.*)

So Doral, a cigarette that was "good for everybody," came out and never really found an audience, although sales were respectable enough. But then RJR redesigned the filtered Camel packs and sales of filtered Camels caught on, enough to threaten Marlboro and enough to push Doral into the backseat of the sales rack. RJR decided to make Doral a generic, and it found its audience among smokers of all ages that was happy with it's flavor and price (about 10% cheaper than Camel or Marlboro.)

This brings us to our next class, **GENERICS.** Generics are brands that are slightly cheaper than Mass Premiums, usually no more than 10-15% cheaper than the leading Masses. For example, if Marlboro Red and Newport Green are selling for 4.99, a Generic like Basic or Parliament would cost about 4.25. (Parliament is another brand that has made the journey from Premium, to Mass Premium, to Generic. Some markets, mainly in the South, sell it as a Sub-Generic, our next class.)

SUB-GENERICS are name-brands that are sold for up to a dollar off of the price of Mass Premiums. Right now, this market is red hot. L&M, Pall Mall (filtered), Marlboro Special Blend, Viceroy, GPC and many others fill the racks attempting to entice Mass Premium smokers away from their regular brands. This market has always accounted for at least 10% of overall cigarette sales, but in the last two or three years they have almost doubled in market share. Many people are simply unwilling to pay the extra price for Marlboro Reds or Newport Greens when there exists a dearth of reasonably-priced smokes that don't taste much different from their regular brands. (We used to have a saying in the cigarette industry that if you give a smoker a carton of a new brand, he'll abandon his former brand and never look back.)

SSG'S (Sub-sub Generics) command the smallest part of the cigarette market share. These are brands that may or may not be manufactured by a major tobacco company. They are not usually promoted (or even acknowledged) by the cigarette manufacturer so as to not tarnish that company's image. (Look at a pack of Pyramids and try to figure out who makes them [Ligett Vector] and then try to imagine what exactly makes them cost a quarter of the price of Marlboros.) All of the major cigarette manufactures make SSG's, whether they wish to admit to it or not.

Silva Thin
the one that's in

Silva THINS

"Us Tareyton smokers would rather fight than switch!"

Tareyton

At the bottom of the dungheap of the cigarette caste system exists the group with no name, the "untouchables," as it were. These cigarettes, if they can even be called cigarettes, are usually nothing more than 100% reconned-recon (floor sweepings of floor sweepings) that are wrapped in paper and have no consistency in taste or production methods.

The reason for this is that small companies buy tobacco crumbs from major companies. These particles are so bad, quality wise, that they can't even make it into SSG's. These small cigarette companies, sometimes comprised of less than 10 employees, remanufacture the particles into sheets of semi-smokeable tobacco that is then sprayed down with liquid casing to give it a somewhat uniform flavor, then they're packaged into cheap paper wrappers. (Just for fun, compare the thickness of say, a pack of Cherokee cigarettes against a soft pack of Marlboro Reds; it's like comparing tissue paper to notebook paper.)

These cigarettes can change flavor from pack to pack. One batch may be constructed from a bunch of leftover Winston scrapings while the next batch is made from leftover Parliament scraps. Some companies even have the audacity to claim that their "Native American" cigarettes are additive free since they're not hosed down with all kinds of ph boosters and whatnot. But I guarantee you that they ceased to be additive free the third, fourth, fifth and twelfth time they were reconned at their original place of manufacture. (Legally, these cigarettes can be touted as "additive free" since the tobacco has only had

final flavor casings sprayed on at the factory, but there's a far cry between **Natural American Spirits** and **All Natural Native** cigarettes [*see below*] aside from just the price.)

The price is another reason that the government is going after the cigar industry thanks to these El-Stinko del Rey Cheapos. Since cigars and cigarettes are taxed differently (cigarettes being taxed almost 75% higher in some states compared to cigars) the manufacturers of these cigarettes have begun to dye the wrap paper brown. TA-DA! Instant cigars. These "little cigars" may trigger the highest tax increase in the cigar industry ever seen, since cigarette smokers can buy these legally, over the internet, for as little as .50 cents a pack. On top of that, they are available in a wide array of flavors, which as we all know, the FDA has a yen for, since flavored tobacco causes third graders to wake up one day and say "Gee, I'm going to skip school today and try flavored tobacco." Damn if it ain't a mess all the way around.

I do wish to point out that not every manufacturer of "little cigars" are rogue cigarette manufacturers trying to bypass tax laws. There are genuine cigar makers that have been making these filtered cigars for decades and I want to stress that these are actual **cigars** and not simply cigarettes in blackface. Winchester, Al Capone, Remington, and Vendetta are brands that I've smoked on occasion and consider to be worthy small cigars that are good for killing time on a lunch break or for quickly stinking up the house when you find out that your mother-in-law is in town for a visit.

So there you go; the entire rainbow of cigarette classes. Premium, Mass Premium, Generic, Sub-Generic, Sub-Sub Generic, and dog droppings. (For sake of brevity I've skipped over the occasional anomalies like Nat Sherman, Bali Hai and Clove-type smokes.) But the "meat" of this article is about answering reader's questions

Hey RJR, instead of going after Swedish Camel and Lucky Strike snus producers, why not protect your assets on the homefront?

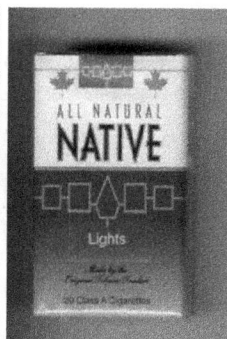

as to what brand is right for them.

First off, I don't encourage smoking cigarettes, and my intake is no more than three a day. Even this is enough to cause lung cancer (trust me, I'm going through chemo and radiation right now). I encourage all of you to switch to smokeless tobacco, or a type of smoking that requires no inhalation like pipes or cigars.

With that out of the way, here's the skinny on today's budget brands. (These are just my opinions based on my ancient experience in the industry.) We have the revitalized brands like L&M and Pall Mall producing good numbers in the Sub category. They're both brands that are familiar to older smokers, but for new smokers, they may not ring a bell.

Pall Mall cigarettes use a pretty crappy blend of tobaccos that taste pretty wicked but burn slow, which many smokers appreciate. Pall Mall smokers are fooled into thinking that they're getting their money's worth, but in all actuality their cigarettes are packed full of recon and re-recon. So you basically have, in Pall Mall, a cigarette that is **packed full** of substandard tobacco. That's why it burns so slow.

On the flip side of the coin you have L&M, which uses a pretty good deal of virgin and premium blended tobacco, with much less recon than other brands in this category. The downside is that since the tobacco is of a good grade, there's much less of it in the cigarette than in other brands. L&M's burn so quickly because there's hardly any tobacco in it! But what tobacco is actually in there is on par with a Mass Premium brand. It does "taste expensive," as the ads say, but you'll need to smoke a 100mm to get anything out of it, and even then it still smokes quicker than a regular, king sized Mass Premium!

So between L&M and Pall Mall, I would say go with L&M if you want quality, and go with Pall Mall if you want quantity. I personally would go with L&M as Pall Malls taste like dookie to me. Also, L&M is about to come out with a "yellow" pack, aka the "Turkish and Domestic blend," which tells you right away that they're gunning for Camel smokers.

The next group of questions I get are all about the Marlboro family. Honestly, I can't keep up with them all. There's Marlboro Brown, Gold, Fusion, Zoetrope, etc. I can't tell the difference between the "special blends," the Blend 27, the Black and Tan, etc. All I can say is that the cheaper the smoke, the cheaper the grade of tobacco that it's probably blended with.

There is, however, a new blend of Marlboro that has caught my attention. It's in a brownish type of label (again with the brown/gold/tan) and it's called Marlboro Southern Cut. Now, it's just hit the market and it's being sold under a "special introductory price," but I have to say- it's the best blend of cigarette tobacco that Philip Morris has come out with since the days of... well, Philip Morris cigarettes.

I recognized the aroma and the blend immediately. After I got home, I performed my homemade alkalinity test (I might make an article about that in the near future) and found that of all the cigarette brands on the market today, the contents of Marlboro Southern Cut are damned near in the area of pipe tobacco. This gives it somewhat of a harsh taste if you're inhaling it, but if you smoke it like pipe tobacco without inhaling, well then you're on to something.

The blend is very high in burley, and has the expected sugary finish associated with lean Virginia tobaccos. I wrote about Half and Half cigarettes and associated "pipe cigarettes" a couple of issues back, and damned if Philip Morris didn't come out with a revamp of the old burley-strong aromatic cigarette.

Back in the late 1800's, smoking tobacco was *tobacco*. There was no "chewing" tobacco or "smoking" tobacco; you either chewed it or you let it dry out enough to smoke in a pipe. Or you ground it into snuff. If it was too dry to chew, you soaked it in molasses for a day or two. But once

Bright leaf tobacco was found to make the smoke so mild that you could actually inhale it, we had a nation of nicotine addicts who began abandoning their pipes for the cheaper and easier alternative: cigarettes.

In fact, the first mass-manufactured cigarettes were nothing but pipe tobacco wrapped up in paper or corn husks. The original Camel cigarette was Prince Albert pipe tobacco wrapped in silk paper. Lucky Strike cigarettes were the same as Roll Cut Lucky Strike tobacco. Bull Durham "manufactured" cigarettes quickly began to outsell the pouched "pipe" variety, and brands like Hedges and Velvet proudly announced on the side of their tins that their tobacco was suitable for both pipe and cigarette smoking.

Philip Morris didn't even bother changing the names of their smoking tobacco. Their "Bond Street" and "Revelation" pipe tobacco packets were almost identical to the cigarettes that carried the same name. By 1940, all bets were off as Philip Morris encouraged their pipe smokers to start inhaling the smoke- since it was "Cool, crisp and mellow- in a satisfying manner known only to cigarette smokers."

I remember smoking Bond Street cigarettes. I remember my dad rolling Bond Street pouched tobacco into cigarettes to take to work with him and when he came home, he would fill his pipe with the same tobacco. I do not recall if he inhaled or not when he smoked cigarettes, but I know that he never inhaled pipe tobacco. "It tastes real rank that way," he once told me.

But by the 1950's, Burley and Bright tobaccos were so mild that you could practically make a cigarette that even a child could inhale without coughing too badly. The aromatic cigarettes made from pipe tobacco that I remembered from my childhood were gone now, replaced with "toasted" Oriental and "Turkish" tobaccos, with a low alkalinity and a high nicotine content. [In my last article] I wrote about the occasional efforts to make a good pipe-tobacco cigarette in the ensuing decades, but they never did catch on like they should have.

Not even a few months go by and here comes Philip Morris with Marlboro Southern Cut. As I've stated, it's kind of harsh when smoked as a cigarette, but with a good cigarette holder you can smoke it like a pipe and you'll have a pretty good idea of what cigarettes *used* to taste and smell like. I've gone through an entire pack and it's been a pretty nostalgic trip for me, even though they're filtered and they come in a box.

So the purpose of this article wasn't to kiss Philip Morris's ass or to promote smoking. It was to let you know that there is a brand of cigarettes out there right now that are manufactured in a manner that this generation has never had the chance to experience.

I still have a few questions about it though. The "Southern" part I get, but the "Cut" isn't any different than your average Marlboro. Maybe PM is trying to differentiate this product from their cheaper "Blend" line, as it should be. From what I can tell, there's very little recon tobacco in it compared to today's cigarettes (even compared to the flagship Marlboro Red brand) and I've ditched my Chesterfields for good. Now when my doctor asks me if I smoke cigarettes, I get to quote Bill Clinton and say "Yes, but I don't inhale." Of course, I inhale every now and again, just like Philip Morris used to urge pipe smokers to do, just so I can be satisfied in a "manner known only to cigarette smokers."

I wonder if PM will dust off their old slogans from Bond Street and Revelation. "Wonderful flavor and aroma... even the ladies approve!" I'd like to have that slogan printed on a T-Shirt, since it's a postulation that I've attempted to equiponderate my entire life.

Well, at least the "aroma" part. (Thanks, Lifebuoy Soap and Clubman shampoo). STE

Bill Johnson told me a joke the other day.
"What did Lincoln say when Booth shot him?" *he asked.*
"I don't know," *I answered.*
"OW! Somebody shot me in the damn head!"

Snake Bit and Shakin'

By Jim Walter

Ask anyone who has ever picked tobacco for a living, and they'll tell you it's probably the most hazardous job they've ever had. Your body is threatened the moment you enter the field. The blinding sun bears down on you all day, which could lead to such short term maladies as heat-stroke or sunburn, or to long term illnesses like skin cancer and respiratory problems.

In the field, you face an onslaught of critter attacks from seemingly innocuous insects like boll weevils, hookworms, dung beetles (which spread bacteria); plus ants, bees, yellow jackets and wasps (which possess stingers and small quantities of neurotoxins.) Perhaps the most dangerous of all is the common mosquito, which spreads malaria and other debilitating diseases. And let's not forget lethal Arachnidia such as venomous spiders (the Black Widow, Wolf Spider, Brown Recluse, etc) and scorpions.

As if these threats weren't enough, even the tobacco plants themselves are toxic and in some cases, fatal to pickers such as the young and the elderly. "Green fever" is a case of nicotine poisoning that results from absorbing rich nicotine through the skin while handling raw tobacco plants. It can cause a severe toxic reaction and in extreme doses, even kill a healthy adult. There's not a tobacco picker I've interviewed that hasn't had at least a mild case of nicotine poisoning in their lifetime. There's really no way to avoid it either; picking and topping tobacco stalks is nigh impossible to do while wearing work gloves. It is for this reason that many states have laws in place that prohibit minors from picking tobacco. I've learned that these laws are almost uniformly ignored by farmers and their families.

But it's a threat to the tobacco plants themselves that helps to bring along what may be the farmer's greatest danger in picking tobacco. Small rodents like mice, chipmunk and gophers love the soil and foliage that a tobacco patch gives them. There's plenty of insects and worms that they can munch on, and it's generally pretty easy for them to escape the eye of humans even while wreaking havoc on the plants and soil.

There is one saving grace when it comes to the rodent population, but it comes at a sometimes perilous price: the humble snake. In areas with the venomous types, they pose just a great a threat to the tobacco worker as they do the rodents (and other snakes) that they feast upon. The purpose of this article is to explore the different types of snakes, both venomous and non-venomous that are known to frequent tobacco fields.

THE TOBACCO BELT

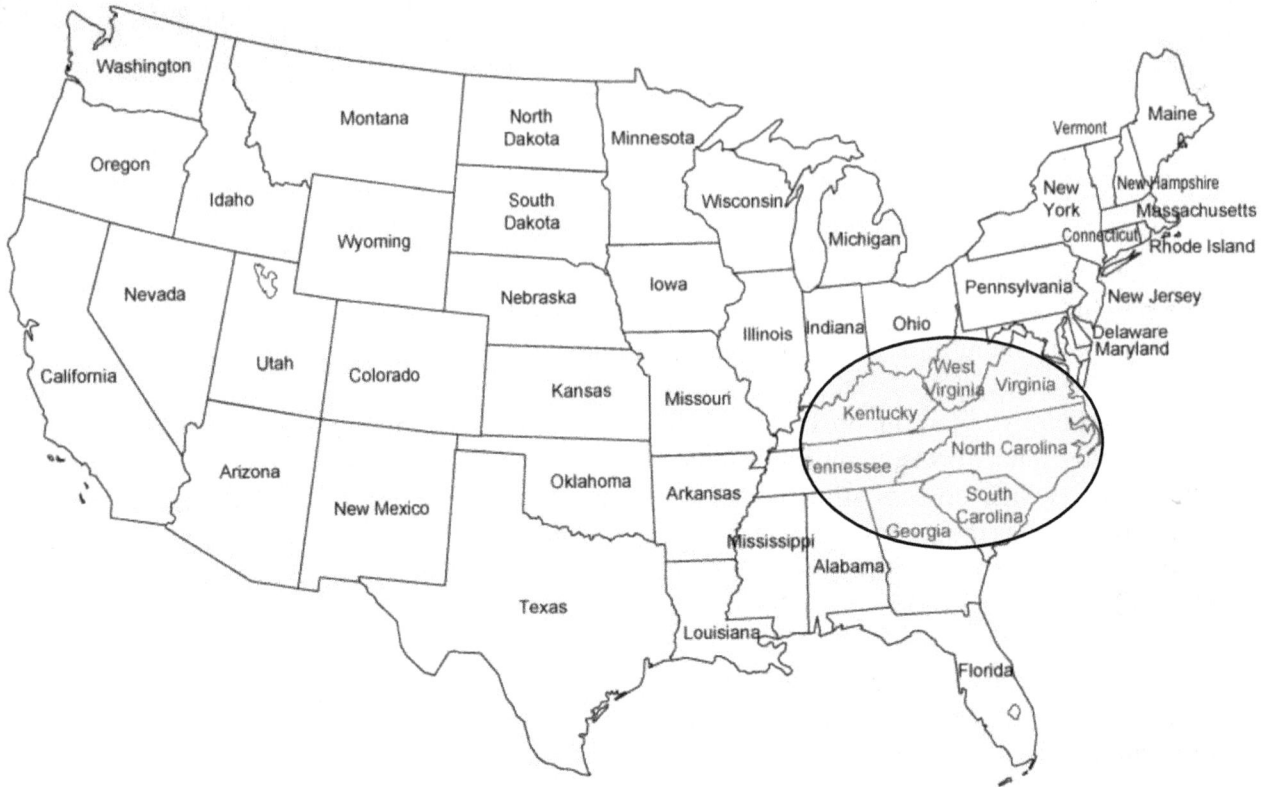

The "Tobacco Belt" is generally thought of as including the states of North Carolina, South Carolina, Kentucky, Tennessee and Virginia and West Virginia at its core, although a great quantity is still grown in Georgia, Northeast Alabama, Southern Ohio and Indiana, and parts of Delaware and Maryland.

The biggest threat to the region's tobacco farmers come from the pit viper family, which includes the Rattlesnake genus (Pigmy, Diamondback, and Canebreak), the Water Moccasin (aka the Cottonmouth), and the Copperhead. (All of the snakes in the pit viper family of North America are split into different sub-genus of territorial proclivity, such as the Eastern/Western Diamondback, Southern/Northern Copperhead, etc. For brevity's sake I've refrained from differentiating between what is essentially the same creature found in different parts of the country.)

The two groups most likely to be bitten by a venomous snake in this region are farmers and inexperienced snake handlers. Of the former, tobacco farmers make up the largest percentage; of the latter, intoxicated, non-professional snake handlers attempting to pick the snake up account for the majority of bites. About 6,000 people are bitten each year, but death occurs in less 1% of all victims. However, toxic bites can leave a long-lasting, and sometimes, ultimately fatal toll on the human body.

As the pictures above and right show, the Water Moccasin (aka the Cottonmouth) can vary in color from a light brown banded pattern to a very dark, almost black appearance. This often leads to confusion from inexperienced snake handlers who often mistake them for non-venomous look-a-likes such as the brown water snake or the common blacksnake.

Cottonmouths share a close DNA to their cousin, the Copperhead, and are usually found within the same areas. For years it was believed that the Cottonmouth was the more aggressive of the two, but in recent years, scientists have come to believe that the Copperhead displays a more aggressive streak. The STE's Bill Johnson, former North Carolina tobacco farmer, explains the difference firsthand:

"You can walk past either snake and not see it. A cottonmouth will usually try to get away, but a copperhead will stand its ground and is much more likely to strike out at you. On the other hand, most of the time a copperhead will leave a dry bite [a bite that does not inject venom into the bloodstream] but it's almost a guarantee that you will be poisoned if bit by a cottonmouth."

The wet, swampy regions that are favored by the two snakes are found from as far north as Delaware and as far south as Florida. Their presence is rare, though not unheard of, in the northern and western states as well. The problem with these snakes is that they are opportunistic feeders, and will eat anything from small rodents to other snakes- even members of their own genus. They are known to coil around the base of the tobacco plant and remain camouflaged, in wait of prey. Unfortunately, the human victim is usually bitten before he sees the snake, either in the hand or arm if he's pulling up the plant, or in the leg or ankle if he's walking past the snake.

"My mother was pulling up a plant one day, and what she thought was a copperhead bit her on the calf," according to Bill Johnson. "We took her to the hospital, but since we didn't have the snake with us, they couldn't administer anti-venom without knowing exactly which snake bit her. They gave her antibiotics for the poison and pain killers. By the next day, her leg had swollen to almost double its normal size, and was dark blue around the bite, almost black."

"We took her back to the doctor and he looked at the wound, and said that he was pretty sure it was a copperhead by the way it had started to spread. He still couldn't administer anti-venom though, for reasons I'm still not clear on. But anyway, we had to go every two days to drain the pus out of her leg and after about two weeks the swelling had gone down. When she was told that all the venom had been flushed out, they had to cut a patch of skin off of her leg that had necrotized which was about a square two inches and about a quarter of an inch deep. I remember that you could see the bone afterward. This was before they did skin grafts, so they just gave her a poultice to keep wrapped up around it, and she wore it for about a year. It got infected several times and there was always talk of amputation, but thank God it never came to that."

Above: the Copperhead, which is often confused with its cousin the Water Moccasin (right). The Water Moccasin gets its nickname "Cottonmouth" from its all-white mouth area, which it flashes as a warning to larger threats.

As Bill explains, even though death by Copperhead /Cottonmouth bite is rare, it can leave permanent scarring and tissue damage even from the most minor of attacks. Anti-venom is rarely administered except in the most extreme cases. Bite victims are usually kept in the hospital for up to 48 hours while their fever is kept under control.

Although the Copperhead/Cottonmouth bite is one that most people walk away from, children and elderly adults aren't usually so lucky. Death is almost a guarantee for these victims if medical intervention is not administered.

Rattlesnakes

The Rattlesnake family is the other genus of pit viper most prevalent throughout the region. Several species are known to exist, all exhibiting similar behavior. Attacks from Rattlers are less common compared to Cottonmouths and Copperheads, possibly due to their hermit-like nature and their ability to warn potential threats with their rattled tail. Rattlesnakes are far more likely to be found in tobacco barns as opposed to tobacco fields, as they prefer a sheltered environment over open spaces.

"I only ever saw one Rattler in my whole life," Bill adds. "I was [in a barn] picking up pieces of wood from the pile to throw in the flue, and I heard the rattle. I got my daddy, who kicked away the wood pile until the snake emerged. He shot it with a shotgun, and that was that." Bill's experience is the most common encounter experienced between man and Rattler.

Though the occasional bite does occur, it is thought to be slightly less toxic than a Copperhead bite. Rattlesnakes tend not to release as much venom as their more ornery relatives, and death from a Rattler bite is almost unheard of in this region.

The Coral Snake

The rarest, but deadliest venomous snake in the tobacco belt is the Eastern Coral Snake. However, it is so reclusive that the likelihood of being bit by one is extremely low. The Coral snake contains more venom than any of the previously listed snakes, and what makes it particularly dangerous is that it is colored very similarly to the harmless King Snake.

Left: the deadly Coral snake and its harmless look-a-like, the Scarlet King Snake (right.) Remember the old adage: "Black and white, it's alright; Black and yellow, kill a fellow."

Though most deaths occur from unknowing people mistaking the Coral for a King Snake, there is an occasional accidental bite that can prove fatal. In 1997, a tobacco farmer in North Carolina was bitten in his field by an Eastern Coral. He died in the hospital three days later.

Speaking of North Carolina, you are three times more likely to encounter a venomous snake in this state than in any other state in the tobacco belt. Herpetologist Dave Moore explains it best: "North Carolina has every type of venomous snake that inhabits North America all in one place. You've got your rattlers, your vipers and even sea snakes, which makes it pretty much a given that eventually you will encounter a venomous snake than you would in a place like Vermont or Delaware."

FLORIDA

Florida has lately started growing more tobacco than in decades past. As the cigar center of North America, it's only natural that leaves for binders, filler and wrap are being cultivated here instead of further south. In addition to all of the aforementioned snakes that also belong to the Tobacco Belt states, Florida has a new problem on its hands: giant Constrictors.

When Hurricane Andrew hit Florida in 1992, hundreds of pet stores were decimated. Pythons and Anacondas escaped into the freedom of Florida's Everglades, where they populated, and now dominate the food chain. These giant snakes are known to eat everything from turtles and alligators to human beings. What's worse is that they are now leaving the 'Glades and encroaching on populated areas. They have even been known to enter homes and reticulate around small children, often killing them in their beds or cribs.

While it remains to be seen how these giant snakes will effect tobacco farmers in the region, an even more ominous threat may hang in the balance. What started as a few isolated sightings in years past has turned into dozens a year; reports of King Cobras stalking the territory near the Everglades are no longer being dismissed as mere confusion: they are actually being caught by wildlife experts. This brings us to our next geographic location...

Asia

Much of the world's tobacco is grown in Asia, including the majority of the tobacco grown for smokeless use, which is grown in India. The continent is host to some of the deadliest snakes in the world, and like other continents, tobacco farmers are especially at risk of running into some of these deadly serpents. More tobacco farmers die of snake bites in Asia than in any other continent in the world.

THE COBRA FAMILY

The Cobra family dominates Asia. The most common, the King Cobra (above left), is relatively docile and is not likely to come in contact with human populations. Though the King Cobra is just as deadly as its brethren, reported bites are fairly rare. This snake would rather retreat than fight a larger foe. Like other members of the Cobra family, the King Cobra's head can expand into a hood shape that is meant to scare off potential predators. The "King" in its name comes from the fact that the King Cobra is the largest of the Cobra family, measuring up to 13 feet in length.

The most common Cobra encountered is the Indian Cobra, aka the Spectacled or Monocled Cobra (below left). It is aggressive and very common, and most deaths occur in India from this type of snake more than any other. It gets its nickname from the "eyes" on the back of its head which help it to scare away predators that may attempt to sneak up behind them.

The Spitting Cobra (below) is the most unique of all Cobras in that its primary defense

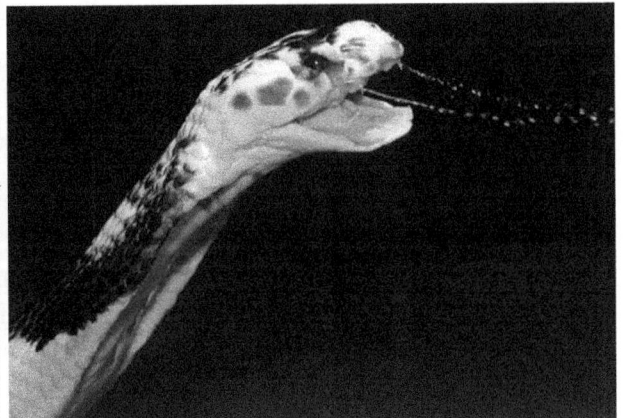

mechanism that consists of firing off a fine stream of venom into its victim's face. This venom temporarily blinds the target and the snake can then retreat or attack, depending on circumstance.

An Indonesian tobacco farmer recounts his experience with a Sumatran Spitting Cobra:

"I was topping off the coronas of the plants when I heard the hissing sound. I looked all around, but couldn't find the snake. Suddenly it was like someone had shot acid into my eyes, and I felt the snake strike twice into my leg, bam- bam. Lightning quick. I never even saw the snake. I was half blind, trying to make it home and I could feel myself getting numb and dizzy, falling upon the ground, trying to scream for help, but my tongue was swollen. My daughter came to my aid and my next memory was of waking in the hospital. The anti-venom saved my life, but I lost the leg." The farmer now wears a plastic prosthetic in place of the amputated limb.

Though he lost his left leg, the farmer is still very fortunate compared to most who are attacked by a Spitting Cobra. Two "wet" bites back to back have been known to kill a full grown man in as little as eight minutes.

THE MANGROVE

The Mangrove is a common venomous snake that likes to hang out in tree limbs and fall upon unsuspecting tobacco pickers.

Thankfully, the bite from a Mangrove is rarely, if ever fatal. The Mangrove's venom is so mild that most bite victims rarely experience anything worse than a migraine headache and flu-like symptoms that last about 48 hours.

THE BLUE CORAL SNAKE

Singapore tobacco farmers have a fear of "the blue death", aka the Blue Coral Snake. The Blue Coral is barely ever seen by the general public, but farmers are almost always the victim of a Coral bite, and 82% of those bites result in death.

The large percentage of deaths can be attributed to the fact that the Coral's venom is especially potent and anti-venom does not exist. They tend to wait under bundled tobacco hands and strike when their cover is removed. Death usually occurs within 8 hours, though some fatalities have been reported within just a few minutes.

Due to space limitations, we've had to hold back the second part of this article until next issue. Stay tuned!

Whiskey, Sex and Snus: The Snuffers That Built America

Part Two

By RW Hubbard

Last issue, we explored the mass exodus of Swedes and Scandinavians that left their homeland for the United States in order to toil in our mines, on our railroads, and with other manual tasks that mainstream America left for immigrants and people of color to work in.

Each culture had one thing in common: their love of snuff. The French, The Germans, The Chinese, the Scotch, the Irish, the Scandinavians, the Poles, the African-Americans, the Russians- they all had their own peculiar flavors and styles of snuff that the other groups found strange, even blasphemous, when viewed in relation to their own habits.

This second part of our article further delves into the historical crucible that forged what may have been the greatest era in all of snuff history; America, the melting pot of humanity, soon grew to be the only nation on earth that catered to every style of snuff used worldwide. While some styles of snuff would become popular and remain so to this day, other styles would be forgotten or left to remain as a curio belonging to a certain sect of immigrants. Let's take a closer look at the pioneers of American industry, and the snuff that represented their cultures and history.

The Men That Built The Railroads

Dick Janson worked the Alaskan frontier for six decades. He was attracted to the high wages offered there. "Most often you made about 3.50 a day then if you were a Swede. If you were a negro or an Irishman, you might could expect about 3.00 a day. If you were Chink [Chinese] you might make as much as a negro, maybe less. This was about twice as high as anywhere else in the country, where the going rate for most labor was around 1.75 a day."

"The railroad was built by what they called 'station men'. These were two or three guys that would band together and form a company, and they would travel and work together. They thought that the larger a company they were, the better rates they could get for pay. Like a union. They followed construction projects from around the world, and they most all knew each other. Most all of us worked at one time at the Gillevara Ofoten, which was the Iron Ore mountain in Sweden. That was the world's farthest north railroad."

In going on to describe the character of these station men, Janson summed up the typical company worker as such:

"A station man is a hard rock man. A rough and ready construction man of the old school. Hard drinking, hard working, cussing, spitting snus, he will tackle any job no matter how tough. There was guys like Long Carl Carlsson, foreman of the Chitina Crossing. He got his name because he was a long, lanky Swede. "

"Most all the workers were Scandinavian, and we give em all colorful nicknames. There was Pickhandle Jones, The Norwegian King, Shoot-em-up Swede, Crooked Swede, Hurry-up Jones and the like. There was Society Kid, whose real name was Price Nettleton. He was fireman for Dan Barret. Big Dan never said much on account that he always had a mouthful of snus, and if he opened his mouth up it would spill out allover."

Some men who came to work on the railroads left with not just a new nickname, but often a new Anglicized surname. The Polish were especially prone to this re-naming:

"If a Mr. Jyrklpotozofosky applied for work, the paymaster would look at him up and down and say something like "You're Mr. Jack Robbins now." And that was that. From that day on he was Jack Robbins whether he liked it or understood it."

A day's work was determined by placement of a case of whiskey. The foreman would go deep into the tunnel to the distance that he wanted the men to work until sundown. There he would hide a case of whiskey behind some rocks, and whenever the men found the hidden stash, they knew that their work was over for the day. The common saying of the time was that the Copper River Railway was built on "Snus, overalls, whiskey and snowballs."

There was only one strike ever recorded in the history of the Copper River Railway. It was a result of a shortage of one of the "four elements" that helped build that railroad. When supply lines choked up and freighters were unable to deliver several thousand pounds of snus, the men refused to work. Jack Heney ended the "Great Snus Strike of 1903" when he personally commandeered a freight train with an entire car loaded with Swedish snus to the scene of the strike. The men went back to work immediately. [See inset for another recorded "snus strike" which took place almost half a century later.]

According to a retired foreman, keeping the men supplied meant providing them with "food, snus, powder, snus, drill steel, snus, shovels, hand tools, and snus." Often, the Swedes would gamble and drink their entire days wage down to the last dime. They were careful to keep that last dime, however, as that purchased a day's ration of snus. Many men regularly went without food in order to fund their snus habit. These workers often made meals from rotten moose meat in order to stay alive.

Rappée Snuff

Among these workmen, "Rappee Snuff" was a generic term for all moist snuff, interchangeable with Swedish, Danish, Finnish, Norwegian, Polish, Estonian, and some Russian snuff- as well as some American brands like Copenhagen (Weyman), Lorrilard, and Garrett.

The term "Rappee" originated from the French "Rapé" snuff sometime in the mid-1600's. Tobacco sold in France came in a foot-long cylindrical roll called a "carrot" (due to its shape). Snuffers would grate the tobacco carrot over the lid of their snuff box in order to pulverize it into a fine powder. The grated lid was called a "rasp", translated from the French "rapé". The French began importing some of this fine cut snuff to other countries, where the word "Rapé" turned into "Rapee", "Rappee" or "Rapée" and became confused with a type of tobacco instead of a style of cut.

"French Rappee" could mean any number of things, from plain grated tobacco, to moist or dry snuff made from light or dark tobacco. Generically though, "Rappee" or "Rapé" was a broad term that described dark, moist snuff that was meant to be taken orally or nasally. P. Lorillard, founder of the oldest American tobacco company still in existence, was the first to import "rappee" snuff into the US. His catalogs described "Lorillard's Imported Rappee snuff, also known as Swedish or Polish wet snuss."

Thus, the origin of "wet" snus can be traced back to the Swedes, who were the first to begin tailoring their snuff recipes into moist, oral tobacco. Each country that they introduced moist snuff to began to make their own version of it, in turn putting their own cultural stamp on the product. The Swedes favored salty, mildly flavored snus that was sold very wet. The Poles and the Russians liked their version of snus to be a bit dryer, but just as plainly flavored. The Austrians, Swiss and Americans that dabbled in "Rappee" snuff tended to prefer bolder, smoked flavors native to their flue or fire curing methods.

British Rappee was usually just as dark and fine as Swedish snus (and as smokey as American brands), but not as moist. In England, oral tobacco use was seen as a custom that

The Halibut Fleet Snus Strike of 1945

By Pat Roppel

courtesy of Capital City Weekly © 2010

Among the various supply shortages plaguing the fishing fleet in the season of 1945, as World War II wound down, was Copenhagen "snoose." Undoubtedly all of the Southeast halibut fishermen felt the effects of the shortage, but it was Alaska's Petersburg fishermen who complained the loudest. That city's newspaper said that Petersburg probably consumed a larger tonnage of snoose per capita than any town in the western hemisphere. The fleet was due to sail May 1 for the annual "halibut-snatching" that lasted 60 to 70 days, but the fishermen discovered that the manufacturers, mostly located in Chicago, had been put under a 10-day embargo: this meant that snoose was not being shipped.

The Seattle fleet owners put in anguished calls to their local senator, Warren G. Magnuson. The latter galloped into action. He yipped and howled around the War Production Board so lustily that the embargo was lifted and rush shipments of snoose were sent to the halibut fleet.

Thus, the fleet sailed on schedule, and as the Petersburg paper said, "The hardy Norsemen, facing into the sunrise, no longer were chanting in mournful numbers: 'No snuff, no fish.'" The reporter added, "Why the Scandinavian fishermen require Copenhagen, snuff, snoose, snuss, Scandihoovian-dynamite, Swedish conditioner-powder, or Swedish brain-food, as it is variously called, is something of a mystery to non-Nordics."

Halibut fisherman Ludvig Akslen of the Coolidge said, "You put it under your tongue like this or you just keep it in your mouth and chew it. But you never sniff it, not if you're a fisherman you don't!"

Said another man: "It's a habit. You got to do something at sea, so you might as well chew snoose. It doesn't go out in the wind and rain like a pipe or a cigarette."

The Copenhagen brand was the most popular form of snuff after it was introduced in 1822. I looked for the words "snoose" and "snuff" in the dictionary to find out the difference between the two words. Snuff originally was powdered tobacco inhaled through the nostrils.

It was very popular among women in the early part of the 1800s and was carried in a small "snuff box." Finally I found the other spelling for snoose is "Snus." It was manufactured and mainly consumed in Sweden and Norway.

Chewing tobacco is a smokeless product and is one of the oldest ways of consuming tobacco leaves and originally used by North and South American natives. Its use was almost universal among the American population during the civil war, on the frontiers, and among farmers, ranchers, fishermen and loggers. It was also produced in twist, the oldest form where leaves were twisted into a rope when green. This form was one of the trade items for the Hudson's Bay Company and probably was available at its forts at Wrangell and Taku Inlet. Another form was plug tobacco that was pressed into a molasses base and also may have been traded.

Loose leaf or "scrap" chewing tobacco is the most popular form. At a market in Wrangell, I asked to see the round cans of chewing tobacco. Copenhagen comes in "snuff" and "long" (loose leaf). Several other brands are available in both forms plus "short." Some have flavors such as apple, orange liqueur, cherry, etc. I bet those old fishermen wouldn't have put up with that!

Not one, however, uses the word "snoose" or "snus." Neither snoose or snus are in dictionaries. I finally found the word "snus" on Wikipedia and learned it is chewing tobacco that included 50 percent water, salt, and sodium carbonate. Then it was fermented. Reynolds Tobacco plans to test the original formula for "snus" in the U.S. market.

Pat Roppel, a 50-year resident of Southeast Alaska, is the author of numerous books about mining, fishing, and man's use of the land. Her most recent book is "Striking It Rich, the History of Gold Mining in Southern Southeast Alaska." She and her husband Frank, now living in Wrangell, continue to explore Southeast's history in their boat, the Twinkle.

[Note: the STE has chosen not to edit this article, though it includes a few mistakes. We found it entertaining as an "outsider's" view of snuff and snus taking.]

was practiced only by the lower class. The British loved Swedish-style snus, but they preferred to take it nasally. Ettan was the best-selling imported snus in both the US and England.

A Snuff For All Seasons

As time passed, American snuff manufacturers noticed the growing market for imported styles of snuff, and began to manufacture their own. The Weyman/Bruton Company (makers of Copenhagen, and later Skoal) and Lorillard practically put the snuff import business in the US in its grave by making their own blends of snuff that closely matched the styles of snuff that were being shipped in from other countries. By the 1930's, imported snuff accounted for less than 7% of the total marketshare of snuff consumed in the US. The American snuff makers targeted specific customers for their brands through advertisement in foreign language newspapers. It wasn't uncommon to see a brand like Horseshoe Snuff advertised in Polish magazines or Swedish "songbooks" (popular sheet music that was issued on a regular schedule.) In an American magazine, it was called "Horseshoe Snuff," while the same brand would masquerade as Horseshoe "Polesnuf" or Horseshoe "Snus" in Polish or Swedish-language newspapers, respectively.

By the 1940's, the hundreds of different snuff blends could be condensed into two types: wet or dry. Dry snuff was prevalent in the southern states, where it was mainly used orally. Wet snuff was popular in the midwest where scores of Nordic immigrants had settled. By the 1960's, 72% of the snuff consumed in the United States was moist. Brands like Copenhagen, Skoal, Key, Viking, Seal and Red Seal were becoming available nationwide. The southern states, by the 1970's, became the largest market for wet snuff, with brands like Happy Days, Skoal and Copenhagen leading the way. Use of traditional dry snuff had dwindled to less than 12% of the marketplace. Whereas it once outsold all other forms of tobacco, dry snuff was now a niche novelty. Few brands, like Railroad Mills Maccoboy snuff, still represented the era of "Rappee" snuff, where its moisture and cut allowed it to be used as an oral or nasal snuff. But aside from DeVoe's Eagle Snuff and Railroad Mills, wet/dry snuff was an anomaly.

1982 saw the largest sale of snuff in the United States since 1941. This was mainly due to crackdowns on cigarette smoking and ramped-up advertising campaigns from the major snuff companies. Musicians and sports heroes plugged Copenhagen and Skoal in television commercials (which had not yet been banned like cigarette ads) and gamesmen, lumberjacks, cowboys, and construction workers alike shared the "macho" image of snuff dipping, just like their hard-working ancestors did. Over in England, coal miners were depicted as the typical snuff taker- hands and faced blackened, only their eyes and shiny metal tins visible in ads for Hedges. Yes, snuff was once again the choice tobacco for men who worked with their hands.

Though the big "smokeless boom" of the early 80's was put to a premature halt by governments, anti-tobacco advocates and health workers who grossly exaggerated the negative health effects of snuff taking, the mental image of burley, hard working men and their snuff tins was firmly entrenched in the American mindset. Until RJ Reynolds unveiled their strange

On the topic of "Snusfornuft"

By Erik S. Hansen

"Snusfornuft" is a Scandinavian term that is comparable to the English term "Horse sense," or common sense mingled with the glean of experience. Erik Hansen describes it fully here, along with its negative connotations among warring Scandinavian countries, as it was a common term during the western railroad boom of the late 1800s when Swedes, Danes, Dutch and Norwegians were forced to stop hating each other and work together.

Snusfornuft is a useful but tricky Scandinavian term. Translated literally, the word is a compound made up of contradictory elements: "snuff" or "snoose," on the one hand, and "reason" or "rationality" on the other. A kind of "snoose smarts," if you will, combining the aboriginal Scandinavian smokeless bad habit with some kind of native intelligence. Who knows, maybe the term evolved from snorting or chewing too much "Scandahoovian dynamite," as it later was called in the logging camps or on the streets of those immigrant enclave "Snoose Boulevards" of immigrant America.

In the modern rendition of the term still used in Denmark today, snusfornuft defines a kind of down-to-earth, if simpleminded, common sense. The word seems to imply matter-of-factness not wholly without virtue. But it's a problematic term. For one thing, there are the obvious overtones of political incorrectness attached to the word and the implication that only men have snusfornuft, or common sense, not women. An added problem is that it seems to be a mildly positive attribute. In Danish, applying snusfornuft means the ability to think like a common man. Or at least those men wise enough to stuff some powdered tobacco leaves up their noses. And how smart can they be?!

Come to think of it, snusfornuft might be the ultimate Scandinavian oxymoron. There is a certain irony in thinking of men made more clever by shoving snoose up their noses … or by putting a pinch between cheek and gum. But there are further complications here, in that 19th Century Scandinavian women were known to take snuff, as well. A physician friend of mine notes that the little cup on the back of our hand, there just where tendons join the thumb and wrist—the little indentation made when you stick your thumb in a motion of hitch hiking—is still called 'the anatomical snuffbox." Presumably, it has the name from the perfect size and shape in which to place powdered tobacco and then snort it up the nose. And yes, women did that too.

Here's the kicker. The Swedes use the word snusförnuft as a not-so-nice adjective describing a woman: a snusförnuftig woman is one who lacks originality. But that's only one definition. The prestigious dictionary of the Swedish Academy actually lists over 150 different variations of hyphenated snus words, including this definition of snusförnuftig by poet Rydberg: 'Reason

Leave it to the Norwegians to get caught in the middle and have to sort out a third meaning. Their definition reflects more a childlike, simplistic reasoning. Even self-indulgent, self-satisfied reasoning. Maybe that's why it took only one Norwegian to scurry off 10,000 Swedes. Or maybe why only Norwegians have ever suggested that, when too many simple minded thinkers are obviously involved in a case way over their heads, they say: "Must be we're holding the national championships in snusfornuft."

Enough doggerel thought. Let's cut to the major distinction. Three different definitions of a word must say something about the nature of these cultures, at least in that simplistic "horse sense" might not always provide a good solution. (Other than maybe in: "Good horse sense stopped him from putting that awful stuff in his mouth!") My question is this: What common trait or training in thinking leading to right action is involved when countries—all of whom once were at each other's throats, slaughtering each other ruthlessly in a manner equaling the ethnic genocide currently found anywhere in the world—what causes whole countries to evolve to the point that they quit the sword and live as peaceful neighbors? Some condition must be at work that goes way beyond snusfornuft.

For some time I wouldn't admit the obvious. I suppose I was embarrassed to reveal my ignorance that middle school kids knew more than me. I didn't have a clue what *phronesis* meant. And I didn't ask.

Turns out, that's just the point. The word, even the concept, has died out completely from our language and culture. It's a Greek word. From Aristotle. A word meaning, greatly simplified, something like "practical wisdom," or using the head and the hand in unison in such a way to inspire admiration and allegiance and integrity. All this in one word and concept. And that's not the whole story. Phronesis also an action word, a transitive verb, with a three part inflection describing the ability to reflect (think) and act (do) while simultaneously delivering change based on a set of carefully considered moral values. This "practical wisdom" isn't merely of the snusfornuft or common wisdom variety, as some interpret it; it's the head and hand together. Aristotle notes that one can't be taught phronesis, but rather one needs an education and then the will to live out that education, to experience and reflect, in order to gain phronesis. It's wisdom born of practice.

Our ancient relatives no doubt could have used a good dose of phronesis on many occasions, it seems, just as we could stand a return to the concept in our own day and age. Maybe we're already seeing it. What with an expectant sense of audacious hope, now as we await the new year, along with the prospect of political change just on the horizon, perhaps we are witnessing a reassertion of phronesis. Why if Swedes and Danes and Norwegians can learn to live with each other, even while weaning themselves of both snus and snusfornuft, what's to stop the rest of us from regaining the high ground and making peace with our enemies around the world?

WEYMAN'S
COPENHAGEN SNUFF

THIS Snuff is packed in 1, 2, 4, 6 and 8 ounce PATENT GLASS TUMBLERS, with air-tight metal covers, which perfectly preserve its delicate aroma. Also in 16 OUNCE GLASS JARS, and 5, 10 and 20 pound fancy Earthen Jars, with air-tight metal covers.

More than fifty years ago the superior quality of this Snuff made for it a reputation that has never been exceled or equalled, and no labor or expense will be spared to maintain the reputation so justly and fairly established.

The "Weyman Process" is exclusively our own, and in our standard brand, "Copenhagen," the superiority of our process is fully demonstrated.

We guarantee all material used by us to be free from all hurtful ingredients.

The testimonials we have received from consumers concur "that this Snuff is unequalled."

WEYMAN & BRO.

This page:

A Copenhagen SNUFF ad from an English language magazine, while a Swedish language pamphlet (next page) advertises Copenhagen SNUS.

Both ads appeared simultaneously in 1915. The English language ad focuses on Weyman's high-quality packaging, while the Swedish ad focuses more on the quality of tobaccos used in the manufacture of Copenhagen. A "premium blend of Tennessee and Kentucky tobacco" was sure to satisfy the most "critical" of snusers.

pseudo-snus in 2005, this image would not be challenged.

No matter what the future holds for snuff, one thing can be certain- there will always be an association with smokeless tobacco and the working man. Or in the words of Big John Johnson, an 1889 railroad worker, "A man ain't a man if he isn't carrying a box of snuff on his person."

Appendix; Further Reading:

Swedish Immigration 1846-1914, Alaska State Archives.

Capitol Weekly, Feb. 3 2010.

Hounds on the Road: The Greyhound Bus Company History, Carlton Jackson. 1984.

The Copper Spike, Lone E. Jansson, 1972.

"Southern Centennial", Gregory Scott, *Downtown Journal* March 2010.

Nina Clark, personal interview at the American Swedish institute, Minneapolis Minnesota. www.americanswedishinst.org

"The Wild Swans", Erik S. Hansen, *Church and Life*, 2008.

A Pinch of Snus, EL Brendel, 1950.

Book of Snuff and Snuff Boxes, Matoon M. Curtis, 1935.

The Search for Ancestors, Barton Hildor Arnold, 2006.

Carl-Werner Petterson, *Swedish - American Genealogist Magazine*, 2010.

BLackguard of the Month:
The Monsanto Seed Company
(With Special Guest Barack Obama)

The Monsanto Seed Company: These words are enough to ignite even the most mellow, liberal, hippy tree-hugger into burning their bras and undergarments. This is because Monsanto is at the forefront of production of Genetically Modified Organisms, or GMOs. Why anyone would be against a technology that has the ability to solve the world hunger problem, we don't know. That's a completely different can of super-sized 12 pound worms that we're not going to open.

But in the face of widespread political opposition and grassroots activism, you would expect a big corporation like Monsanto to open up a line of communication and educate the people as to the positives of their work and to try and keep a public image that shows them to be a friend to the poor, the hungry, and the farmers who toil in the sun for years growing Monsanto-created foodstuff.

But what did Monsanto do instead? It further painted itself as an evil monster giant corporation who doesn't care about its customers, its growers, or public perception. You see, Monsanto owns a number of patents on different types of seeds. As with all seeds, they've been scattered and mixed into batches of other seeds, unintentionally or not. When the farmer goes to the seed warehouse to purchase, say, 100 bushels of corn seed, he may or may not have a bushel that has been cross-pollinated with trademarked, patented Monsanto seeds.

Within the last few years, Monsanto has furiously hunted down small farms (especially those that grow tobacco, corn, and wheat) whose seeds contain trace amounts of Monsanto DNA. They are suing small farms at an alarming rate with a goal of shutting down these unfortunate farmers who had the horrible misfortune of inheriting patented Monsanto seed.

So how does the trademarked seed wind up in a non-Monsanto authorized farm? Usually it's the result of a mixup at the seed warehouse. Other times, it's simply nature at work, blowing seeds from one farm to another. In one instance, a truck carrying Monsanto seeds crashed off of the highway and spilled seeds at the edge of a wheat farm. Even though the seeds were for corn, and they weren't growing, and were only found in the patch of field where the truck wrecked, Monsanto successfully sued the small farm in question until the farmer ran out of money (after he had already dumped $200,000 in legal fees) to the point where he could no longer afford to operate the farm that had been in his family's name for three generations.

President Obama (who has been "gifted" millions of dollars from Monsanto, and in turn has filled prime political positions with Monsanto employees) has taken great pains to assure that Monsanto continues to operate unchecked by signing two "Monsanto Preservation Acts" into law. (Quick digression: Secretary of State Hillary Clinton once worked for Rose Law, Monsanto's legal aid. Obama also appointed Elena Kagen to the Supreme Court. She was Monsanto's lawyer during the earliest seed lawsuits. Obama's three largest financial backers in 2008 were Goldman-Sachs, Bill Gates and George Soros, who all own between $500,000 and $900,000 apiece in Monsanto stock).

The first law bars anyone from suing Monsanto for producing GMO crops which may or may not cause health problems down the road in some consumers. Later that year, he passed a second law barring farmers from pre-emptively suing Monsanto over unfair lawsuits, effectively leaving 2 million US farmers open to the same type of harassment Monsanto has been dishing out with a vengeance, in order to "protect" its assets.

Since Monsanto's founder was a Knight of Malta, and since President Obama calls himself a Christian, we thought it wise to end with a message from Galations:

> "Do not be deceived. God is not mocked, for whatever one sows, that will he also reap."

STE

48

FROM THE ARCHIVES

Quite possibly the most requested title that we've had for our "From the Archives" feature, *Tobacco Leaves: Being a Book of Facts For The Smoker* by William Augustine Brennan has been out of print for 100 years. Released in 1914, it is probably the most informative, best-researched and best written of all tobacco literature, both modern and historic.

The subtitle is a bit of a misnomer; equal space is given both to smokeless tobacco and the combustible type. In fact, it covers every conceivable topic and subtopic that a tobacco enthusiast could ever hope to find assembled in one place, moreso than any other book before or since. The book is essentially split into two parts: the first half relates to the history, production and scientific data related to tobacco. The second half is comprised of single chapters dedicated to the finished product. There is a chapter for snuff, pipes, cigars, cigarettes, etc. In this issue, we've reprinted the first half of the book; the second part will be featured in our next issue.

What makes this document so unique is that it was written during the most pivotal era in modern tobacco history, the years 1913-1915. A mere 25 years before the book was written, most tobacco consumed in the US was in the form of plug chewing tobacco. Snuffing was dying out in the Northern states, but the poor population of the Southern states had taken to "dipping" the stuff, whether it was moist or dry. The price of cigars made them a novelty for most smokers; pipe smoking was more common. Cigarettes were all but unheard of to most Americans.

Flash forward ten years and a more prosperous nation had all but abandoned smokeless tobacco. Cheap cigars were the most popular tobacco product on store shelves. The pipe was on the wane. The busier, more industrialized urban populace needed something more convenient to smoke than a pipe while they tinkered away at assembly lines and modern construction projects. While cigarette smoking was prevalent throughout Europe, it wasn't until the first World War that Americans discovered the "perfect" smoking product. Cigarettes were cheaper than cigars, could be hand-rolled with over the counter pipe tobacco, and took only minutes to smoke. Best of all, the light tobacco could be inhaled for an excellent nicotine hit, and there was no stinky odor to offend the ladies like the lingering aroma of cigar smoke. You could smoke one in the rain, in the wind, heck-even in open pitted airplanes 10,000 feet in the air! Cigarettes also appealed to women, who smoked in order to maintain their figure. (In most states, it was illegal for a woman to smoke a pipe or cigar in public. No such restrictions, yet, existed for cigarettes.) The cigarette was the spark, so to speak, that ignited the new tobacco smoking revolution that was just as important a symbol of the roaring 20's as Model T's and It Girls.

But this book was written in that transitional period that bridged the gap between the "old ways" and the exciting new "flapper" style. Very few encyclopedic-style tobacco tomes graced the shelves in those days. Information about tobacco that did exist was usually culled from older books and studies written in the previous century. Brennan used the most up-to-date facts and figures that he could find at the time, in an era before Google and Wikipedia that required years, sometimes decades, of fact collection and data processing on the part of the author. In fact, the references that are cited at the end of each chapter can be viewed as a "must read" checklist for any student, author, or collector of tobacco literature.

Left and Right:

The Cover and Frontispiece from the 1915 reprint edition.

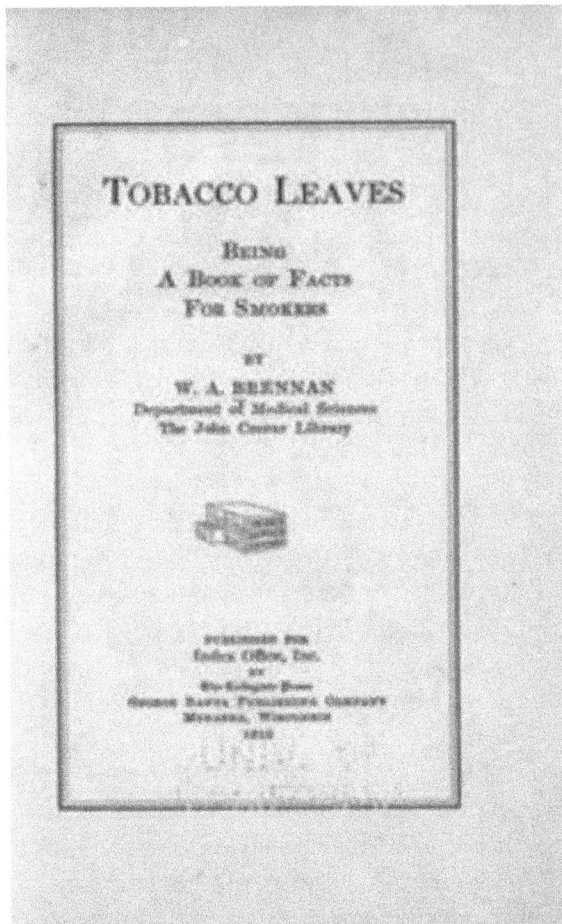

Little is known about the author. Some sources claim that he was a Harvard professor; others that he was a Methodist pastor. The hardcover edition lists "Department of Medical Science, The John Crerar Library." If he ever wrote any other books about tobacco, they have yet to turn up. The publication date on our copy of *Tobacco Leaves* was 1914; the Library of Congress lists it as being published by the Collegiate Press of Menasha, Winsconsin in 1915 with the copyright belonging to W.A. Brennan, born in 1867. This would have put him at around age 47 when he published the book.

A note about our reprinting. This version, dated a year earlier than its hardcover edition (available free online through such websites as the Gutenberg project and Google books) was scanned page by page by Ms. Ellan Wayne, who graciously lent us her copy to use as a reference. It is unknown whether there are any textual differences between the first printing and the later printing, aside from the References section at the end of each chapter. The paperback edition lists them all in one chapter towards the end of the book, whereas the hardcover edition lists them at the end of each chapter. We've gone ahead and copied the format of the hardcover edition, which I believe is easier to comprehend in this format. We have omitted the Index at the end of both editions. This section can be viewed at the above-referenced websites.

But enough of this extended pre-amble. Discover for yourself the difference between Red Burley and White Burley and why fire-cured tobacco makes for poor smoking. Then be sure to join us next month as we conclude our reprinting of this most excellent of reads.

The STE Research Team

TOBACCO LEAVES

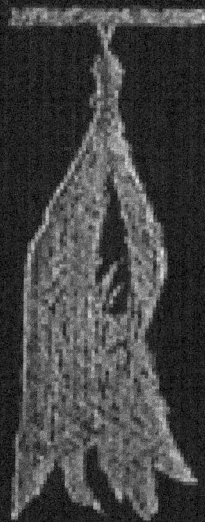

BRENNAN

Introduction

Chapter I
Historical, Botanical.

Chapter II
The Cultivation of the Tobacco Plant.
Climatic and soil conditions—Treatment of the growing plant—Shade grown tobacco—Harvesting.

Chapter III
Production of Tobacco.
Countries which produce tobacco and amount—Production in the New World other than in the United States—Varieties.

Chapter IV
Production of Tobacco in the United States.
Total production—Amount produced by the different States—Varieties raised—Description of the different varieties.

Chapter V
The Chemical Composition of the Tobacco Plant.
Organic and inorganic matters contained in tobacco and the part they play—Analysis of various tobaccos—Nicotine.

Chapter VI
The Curing of Tobacco Leaf.
Objects of curing—Methods.

Chapter VII
The Marketing and Sale of Tobacco Leaf.
Methods of disposal by the grower—The warehouse system—Direct purchase—Principal markets in the United States—Prices.

Chapter VIII
Rehandling and Fermentation of Tobacco Leaf Prior to Manufacture.
Selection of leaf—Treatment and blending—Objects and methods of manufacturers fermentation—Action of microbes.

Chapter IX
Manufactured Products of Tobacco in the United States.
Statistics of production and consumption—Amount of capital invested—Number of plants, etc.

This little book is intended for the man who uses tobacco. While there is a very extensive literature concerning tobacco, yet it is surprising how few books there are written expressly for the smoker. Much has been written concerning culture, production and manufacture; the historical and anecdotal aspects have been catered for; pamphlets and books abusing and denouncing the use of tobacco are plentiful; but the smoker will find it difficult to get a book just giving him the facts concerning tobacco and smoking, which he ought to know, and omitting matters, which, although interesting, are not necessary. This little book is an attempt to fulfil that purpose; and it is felt that no apology is needed for its appearance. If the average user of tobacco is questioned concerning the matters treated in the following pages, he will be found ignorant of them. This ought not be so. The custom of tobacco smoking is so general and so intimate a part of the daily life of the great majority of men, that a better acquaintance with the plant, its qualities, uses and effects, should be cultivated and welcomed.

No claim is made for originality. The facts here stated have been gathered from various sources and the only credit claimed is for putting them together in a concise and consecutive form. The object aimed at is to give information. Whether the custom of tobacco smoking is desirable, whether in any individual case it would be beneficial or otherwise to smoke—these and similar questions are left to the reader's own judgment from the facts and opinions presented, as well as from his own observations. The man who uses tobacco daily should know what he is doing. If statements are made either verbally or in print concerning the custom he should be able to verify them or show that they are incorrect. It is trusted that the information given in these pages will enable him to form a clear judgment whatever the judgment may be.

It may be felt that many aspects of the use of tobacco and matters connected with it have either not been touched on, or only referred to very briefly. The reader who may desire further information will find it in the bibliographical references given throughout the book. These references have generally been consulted by the author and his indebtedness is acknowledged here.

CHAPTER I: HISTORICAL—BOTANICAL

HISTORICAL

The history of tobacco commences with the discovery of the New World by Columbus. The Chinese claim that it was known and used by them much earlier, but there appears to be no evidence to support this claim. Columbus found the natives of Cuba smoking the dried leaves, and his followers are said to have brought the plant to Spain about 1512. Oviedo published a book entitled *La Historia general de las Indias* in Seville in 1526, in which he mentions pipe smoking. It may be inferred that this custom was well established in Spain then.

Sir Walter Raleigh is usually credited with having brought tobacco to England for the first time from Virginia in 1586; and the Virginian Colonists are known to have cultivated the plant at that time; but there is evidence enough to show that Sir Francis Drake was the first to introduce the plant into England. Drake's voyages were made between 1570 and 1580 and he brought the plant with him in one of these. Some give the date of introduction by Drake as 1560. Raleigh was, however, probably the first English distinguished smoker, and he cultivated the plant on his estate at Youghal, Ireland. There is no doubt about the culture of tobacco by the early English Colonists in the U. S., but it is doubtful whether the plant was introduced by them from England or whether they continued a culture learned from the Natives. From Virginia it spread to the other colonies. In Peru and other parts of South America the growing of tobacco was well established at the time of the Spanish Conquest.

In 1560 Jean Nicot, the French Ambassador at Lisbon, sent some tobacco to Catherine de Medici as a cure for headache. Catherine was pleased with it and is said to have become quite addicted to its use. Tobacco was designated the "Queen's herb" and the "Sovereign herb" from this circumstance and Nicot himself is perpetuated in the word "Nicotine" and its derivatives.

Many persons erroneously give credit to Nicot for the introduction of tobacco into Europe. It is quite clear, however, from Oviedo's book, quoted above, that the plant was known in Spain very much earlier; and it is most probable that the immediate followers of Columbus brought samples of the leaves and pipes back to Spain with them. Moreover, in 1558, Phillip II of Spain sent Francisco Hernandez, a physician, to investigate the resources, etc., of Mexico, and on his return he brought back tobacco as one of the products, and grew it as a drug. From Spain and England, the use of tobacco spread by degrees all over the known world.

REFERENCES:

Penn, W. A. *The Soverane Herbe; a history of Tobacco. Chapters I, II.* London and New York, 1901.

Bouant, E. *Le Tabac; culture et industrie.* Paris, 1901.

Shew, Joel. *Tobacco; its history, nature and effects on the body and mind. Wortley,* 1876.

Billings, E. R. *Tobacco; its history, varieties, culture, etc.* Chapters II, IV. Hartford, Conn., 1895.

Comes, O. *Histoire, geographie, statistique du Tabac. Son introduction et son expansion dans tous les pays depuis son origine jusqu' à la fin du XIX siècle.* Naples, 1900.

Fairholt, F. W. *Tobacco; its history and associations.* London, 1876.

Wolf, Jakob. *Der Tabak und die Tabakfabrikate.* Chapter I. Leipzig, 1912.

BOTANICAL

Tobacco belongs to the family of plants known in botany under the name of Solanaceæ. Other well-known members of this family are the Irish potato, the red pepper, the tomato, the egg-plant, etc.

American tobacco belongs almost exclusively to that group of this family which comprise the genus Nicotiana. Of this genus there are about 50 separate species, one of which, Nicotiana Tabacum, supplies almost all the tobacco of commerce. Plants of this species grow from 2 feet to 9 feet in height; they have numerous wide-spreading leaves sometimes as much as 3 feet in length; these leaves may be oval, oblong, pointed, or lanceolate in shape, and are generally of a pale green color when young; they are arranged alternately in a spiral on the stem; the root is large and fibrous; the stem is erect, round and viscid, branching near the top.

The alternate arrangement of the leaves on the stalk, succeeding each other spirally, so that the 9th overhangs the 1st, the 10th the 2nd, and so on, is very characteristic. The distance on the stalk between the leaves is about 2 inches. Flowers are in large clusters, with corollas of rose color, or white tinged with pink. The leaves and stalks are covered with soft downy hair. The plant is perennial but crops are usually raised from seed.

Of this species (N. Tabacum) there are probably more than 100 varieties grown in the U. S. alone. Some of the best known will be described later.

To this same species (N. Tabacum) Havana, East Indian and European tobaccos principally belong. The other important species are:

Nicotiana Persica. Grown in Persia. This has a white flower and the leaves almost enwrap the stem. It is used almost exclusively as a pipe-smoking tobacco. Some claim that this is only a variant of N. Tabacum.

Nicotiana Repanda. This is a species of Cuban tobacco entirely different from that grown in the Havana district. It is also called Yara.

Nicotiana Rustica. A kind of wild growing tobacco principally cultivated in Mexico, and which is claimed as the parent of some of the Turkish, Syrian and Latakia tobaccos although many authorities claim that these tobaccos belong to the species N. Tabacum. The European tobacco is hardier than the American parent plant. The leaves are smaller.

N. Rustica. Also includes common Hungarian and Turkish tobaccos. There are large and small leaved varieties.

N. Crispa. Grown in Syria and largely in Central Asia. Used as a cigarette tobacco in the Orient.

It has been stated above that there are many varieties of N. Tabacum in the U. S. Of these the most important are known to botanists by the names, **Nicotiana Tabacum Macrophylla** and **Nicotiana Tabacum Angustifolia.**

Maryland tobacco belongs to the **Macrophylla** variety and there are many other types differing from each other according to shape of the leaf, size of the stalk, etc.

Virginian tobacco is of the **Angustifolia** variety, and of this also there are many different types.

Most European and other grown tobaccos have been raised from original plants of the Maryland and Virginian varieties.

It should be remembered that there is no essential difference in cigar, pipe smoking or cigarette tobaccos. The differences are physical only. All kinds may be obtained from the same species or even the same variety of the species by suitable culture and crossing.

REFERENCES

Anastasia, G. E. *Le varietá della Nicotiana Tabacum.* Scafati, 1906.

Comes, O. *Delle razze dei tabacchi.* Naples, 1905.

Killebrew, J. B. and Myrick H. *Tobacco leaf; its culture and cure, marketing and manufacture.* Part I. New York, 1897.

Lock, C. G. W. *Tobacco growing, curing, and manufacturing.* Chapter I. London and New York, 1886.

Wolf, J. *Der Tabac.* Chapter II. Leipzig, 1912.

Billings, E. R. *Tobacco; its history, varieties, etc.* Chapter I. Hartford, Conn., 1875.

CHAPTER II: THE CULTIVATION OF THE TOBACCO PLANT

Climatic and Soil Conditions. Treatment of the Growing Plant. Shade Grown Tobacco. Harvesting.

THE CULTIVATION

A few general facts concerning the culture of the tobacco plant and its treatment until it reaches the hands of the manufacturers will be of interest for the smoker.

The general principles underlying the culture of tobacco are the same whether it is intended for the cigar, pipe smoking or cigarette trade; but the treatment of the leaf after it is harvested differs considerably.

Tobacco is a perennial plant. It is, however, usually raised each year from seed. The seedlings are usually ready for planting towards the end of May and are generally planted between the last week in May and the middle of June.

The successful raising of tobacco depends on four principal factors: (1) the climate, (2) the nature of the soil, (3) the seed, and (4) on the method of culture.

The climate must be such as to favor rapid growth and therefore must furnish sufficient heat and moisture during the time the plant is growing. The fineness of the texture and the elasticity of the leaf depend on the climate.

On the soil the plant depends for its food, and for the absorption of those chemical constituents on which depend the burning qualities, the strength and the color.

The physical qualities of the plant, structure and form, thickness of veins, size, shape and distribution of leaves, are derived from the seed.

Finally, on the method of cultivation (including the curing process) depends in part the final color, flavor and aroma; the type and trade value; that is to say, on successful culture and harvesting and treatment at the right time and in the best way, must depend the grower's hopes of the final value of his crop. The quantity of nicotine, essential oils, etc., on which flavor and strength depend, is regulated to the greatest extent by the time of cutting.

The nature of the soil is a very important matter in the culture of tobacco, for the color of the cured tobacco leaf depends almost entirely on the soil. The light colored leaf is grown on light colored soil and the darker leaf is grown on heavy, dark soil. The best type of soil for the raising of tobacco intended for the cigar trade is a warm, deep, sandy loam which rests on permeable well-drained subsoil. The very light colored yellow tobacco cannot be raised except on light colored, porous soils; and so susceptible is this matter of the coloring of the leaf that it has been noted that the darkening of the soil by a liberal allowance of stable manure will, on a very light colored soil, change the color of the tobacco leaf from a bright yellow to a mahogany shade. Very light sandy soils or very light loams with clayey subsoils are usually chosen for these light yellow tobaccos. Although by processes subsequent to growth it is possible to darken the color of tobacco leaf, there is no known process that will make a dark leaf light in color.

Moreover, the soil must be very fertile and rich in the special substances needed by the growing plant. This is all the more necessary because tobacco is a rapidly growing plant, and reaches its maturity within a few months after its planting. The rapidity of growth therefore demands a rich fertile soil well stored with plant food. Good manuring, or liberal treatment with fertilizers, is essential for keeping such soils in prime condition, because the period of growing must not be extended.

Tobacco is usually planted in rows, the rows being from three to four feet apart, the usual arrangement being that the plants are generally about 12 or 18 inches apart in the row. Some planters, however, give the plants more room for many reasons, varying the distance between the plants even as much as 30 inches. Cigar leaf tobacco plants are usually placed about 14 inches apart.

There are various operations necessary during the growth of the plant. The most important of these for our purpose are those known as "priming" or "thinning out" and "cutting." Priming is usually done when the plant is well advanced in growth, but the time varies with different growers and according to the species. It consists in removing the lower or imperfect leaves from the plant, or these which have in any way become injured from insect or other harmful agencies. As a general rule the larger the number of leaves there is on a plant the lower is the quality of the subsequently cured leaf. An average of about 10 leaves to each plant is what is favored by most growers, and the plants are usually

thinned to this extent. Seed buds are removed also at the same time and for the same reason. If the plants are "thinned" late and when they are approaching full growth the leaves removed are not destroyed, but are cured separately and sold as inferior quality and are usually called "primings" or "planters lugs."

In the Southern American States the time allowed for the growth and maturing of the plant is somewhat longer than in the eastern and more northerly states where the soil, owing to richer fertilization, favors the rapid growth. Moreover, a stronger quality of tobacco is wanted and the extra time allows the plant to effect a greater elaboration in its cells of the oils and gums, etc., which contribute particularly to strength and flavor.

Shade Grown Tobacco.

The matter of rapid growth has, however, its limitations. Too much sunlight is considered a disadvantage. Under such powerful action, nutrition is drawn quickly from the soil and the plants ripen too quickly. Under such circumstances the leaves tend to become heavy bodied and not very large in size. To defeat this tendency and produce large, thin silky leaves for the cigar trade, the grower sometimes covers his field with a tent of cheese-cloth or similar protection from the glare of the sun. The ripening process is thereby slowed and the leaves are thinner, larger and lighter in shade. This method is employed principally in Cuba, Florida and Connecticut where cigar wrapper leaves are produced, and such tobacco is known as shade-grown.

Tobacco which has been planted out at the end of May or early in June is usually ready for harvesting at the end of August or beginning to middle of September. The actual time of harvesting varies a good deal according to the variety grown and the physical condition concerned in the growing of the plant. The heavier tobaccos which are intended for the export trade are usually harvested late. The most important operations connected with the culture of the tobacco leaf are the "yellowing" and "curing" processes, and, as these commence with the cutting of the plant, this latter must be done under strictly favorable conditions in order to insure proper results. The cutting must not be done while the sun is very hot, or while there is rain, or before the plant is fully matured.

On the other hand, after the plant has reached its maturity, it must not be allowed to continue its growth, which along with other things would be likely to increase its nicotine content which is not desirable. The experienced tobacco grower knows well from the appearance of the plant when it is best fitted for cutting. The leaves become thick and heavy and assume a drooping appearance. They become crisp with a tendency to break easily, and a mottled, spotty look is noticeable on them.

The surface becomes gummy and oily; the oily substances increases and exudates as the days pass. When these signs appear the tobacco is cut on the first day when the weather favors. It is usual in most cases to split the stalks down the middle and allow the leaves to wilt, before the stalk is entirely cut through. After sufficient wilting the leaves are gathered in piles and exposed to the action of the sunlight; or they are stuck by the stalks on poles or framework and so exposed that the sun and air have free access to all parts. This is the best and most approved practice. "Yellowing" of the leaf is very rapid after the plant is cut; it is the natural effect due to cutting off the food supply of the leaf and the consequent slow death of the vitality of the cells.

It must be remembered that the leaves are large, varying in size (according to species) from 12 inches to over 2 feet in length. Such a leaf needs a large quantity of food and the sudden cutting off of the supply effects a rapid change in appearance. The leaves are allowed to hang on the scaffolds 3 to 5 days until they are fully yellowed. They are then ready for the process of "curing," which is the most important operation connected with cultivation. The "curing" and "fermentation" which the leaf undergoes are chemical actions and their success depends on the proper method of "yellowing." The leaves must not be exposed to the sun too long, because the cells would lose their vitality too rapidly and be unfitted for the new part they have to play in the curing process. The chemical changes will be explained in subsequent chapters. It is desired that the reader should understand that to ensure a successful final issue the planter has need to watch continuously and to know all the conditions. If the leaf does not "yellow" properly no amount of after care in curing will make up for this deficiency. In tobacco growing as in everything else, to ensure final high quality each step in the process must be executed with skill, care, and judgment.

The yield of tobacco per acre varies from about 300 lbs. of leaf in the southern states to 1,000 lbs. or more in the eastern. 700 to 800 lbs. per acre is considered a good average crop.

REFERENCES

Killebrew and Myrick. *Tobacco leaf; its culture and cure, marketing and manufacturing.* Part I. New York, 1897.

Billings, E. R. *Tobacco; its history, varieties, culture, etc.* Chapter XIII. Hartford, Conn., 1875.

Laurent, L. *Le tabac; sa culture et sa préparation production et consommation dans les divers pays.* Paris, 1900.

U. S. Dept. of Agriculture. Farmers' Bulletins Nos. 6 and 60: Tobacco.

U. S. Dept. of Agriculture. Bureau of Plant Industry. Bulletin 96: Tobacco breeding.

CHAPTER III: THE WORLD'S PRODUCTION OF TOBACCO

Total production. Countries which cultivate tobacco. Production in the New World other than in the United States.

THE WORLD'S PRODUCTION OF TOBACCO

The world's recorded annual crop of tobacco leaf is over one million tons. The latest government figures available are those for 1912 and 1913, and show 2,696,401,379 and 2,722,190,030 lbs. respectively. Of this amount Asia and America produce each about 350,000 tons, Europe about 250,000 tons and the rest of the world the balance.

The details of the production in the U. S. will be given in the next chapter.

The principal Asiatic countries which produce tobacco are China, Japan, Afghanistan, India, Persia and Asia Minor. China has an immense production and consumption of tobacco, a large portion of which finds its way into western markets for the cigar and cigarette trade and is sold as "Turkish" tobacco. No figures as to production are available.

British India and Afghanistan produce good tobacco, a lot of which is used in Hindustan and other Eastern countries.

The Persian crop is known to be large, but there are no available records of it. In Persia most of the tobacco raised is of the species known as Nicotiana Persica. This is generally known under its trade name of Tumbach or Tumbeki (or more correctly Teymbeki). This is the common Eastern name for tobacco. It is considerably exported to the countries in the neighborhood of Persia and is smoked in the pipe known as the Narghilli. In this pipe the teymbeki burns in contact with a piece of incandescent charcoal. The smoker draws the vapor through a flexible tube which passes to the bottom of a water chamber and passes above it, whence it is inhaled. The narghili is technically a water pipe. The teymbeki is very strong in nicotine, containing up to 5 or 6 per cent.

Japan produces large and medium size leaf of good color but poor in quality. It is generally used for pipe and cigarette trade.

Nicotiana alata (Regina Noptii): Sometimes erroneously called *Nicotiana persica*, is a floral type of Nicotiana plant that is used for ornamental purposes rather than for consumption.

The real *Nicotiana persica* resembles Tabacum (next page) and is called Tumbach, Tumbeki and Teymbeki in Arabic and was the most commonly smoked and snuffed strain of tobacco throughout the Middle East at the turn of the last century. It was very harsh, and was almost exclusively smoked through a narghile (water pipe or hookah). The smoke passed through the water first, which mellowed and cooled the smoke so that the smoker could inhale it sans the rough kick that genuine *persica* is famous for.

Later, as Turkish tobacco became more in demand, the Arabs began to blend the Turkish and Persica strains in order to make a milder smoke which could be rolled into cigarettes or kreteks.

Today, many types of tobacco seeds and plants that are classified as "Turkish" tobacco are in reality the genetic offspring of Turkish and Persica hybrids that date back to the early 1900s. Sometimes called "Red Turkish", this tobacco is often used in the production of Indian smokeless tobacco and is sometimes exported for use in European pipe tobacco. It is almost completely ignored in the United States due to its harsh flavor, pungent aroma, and difficulty in accepting flavor casing.

The statistics of production for Asia are extremely unreliable. When we consider the teeming populations of China, India and other Eastern countries and the prevalence of the smoking habit, it is very probable that the figure of production (350,000 tons annually) is much under the mark. There is very little export of tobacco from the United States or Europe to the East. Whatever tobacco is consumed there is mostly of its own production.

European Production of Tobacco

In Europe the principal tobacco producing countries are Germany, France, Austria, Russia, Italy and Turkey.

Germany has nearly 40,000 acres under tobacco cultivation in Rhenish Bavaria, Baden, Hesse, and Alsace-Lorraine. The annual production is about 50 to 70 million lbs.; and in addition nearly 3 times that much is imported. German home grown leaf is medium to large in size, of fair body, heavy and with coarse veins. It is used for cigar filler and pipe, but is not suited for cigar wrappers. (See the chapter on cigars.)

French tobacco is raised from Virginia seed. It is dark, coarse and heavy and is suitable for plug and snuff making only.

Russia is the largest European producer. Russian tobacco leaf is very large in size and like the French is coarse, dark and heavy and is only fit for plug and snuff making. There is a lighter kind grown from Turkish seed in South Russia which is fit for cigarettes.

Italy has made several attempts to cultivate good tobacco, and several different types are produced. A dark heavy leaf is grown from Virginia seed, and a type from Kentucky seed is also produced. These types are suitable to the dark, heavy fertile soils of Middle and North Italy. In the lighter sandy soil of the south, the varieties grown are raised from Turkish seed and are similar in appearance and quality to the genuine Turkish tobacco.

Hungary is a heavy grower of tobacco and produces some of the best in Europe. There is a heavy dark type, of a rich brown color, medium sized leaf with small and thin veins, which is used in cigar manufacture. A small bright yellow leaf is also grown, poor in quality and aroma, which is used for pipe smoking and cigarettes.

The most important foreign tobacco as regards U. S. consumers is that known as Turkish. The leaves of the Turkish tobacco are small (about 8″ long), clear yellow in color, and have a special aroma, which renders them peculiarly suitable for the manufacturing of cigarettes. The principal producing centers are Macedonia, Albania, Syria, Palestine and Trebizond, that raised in Macedonia being perhaps the most celebrated. Just like the Cuban leaf, the very best grades of Turkish tobacco are not exported, but are kept for domestic consumption.

Latakia tobacco is produced in the northern part of Syria. This tobacco has a very small nicotine content. It is produced by a special fabrication and is in very great demand as an ingredient of pipe smoking mixtures.

The District of Cavalla in the Province of Roumelia, is one of the most important tobacco centers in the Turkish Empire. There are about 75,000 acres under tobacco cultivation and the annual production is about 10,000,000 lbs. The American Tobacco Co. has a large establishment here through which it purchases its Turkish leaf, amounting to over 6 million lbs. yearly, for the manufacture of Turkish cigarettes, etc.

The total importation of Turkish leaf into the United States during 1913 was:

From Turkey in Europe: 10,816,048 lbs.

From Turkey in Asia: 18,955,295 lbs.

Greece and the Balkan States produce tobacco which partakes of the qualities of Hungarian and Turkish, the Grecian leaf being used a good deal as a substitute for genuine Turkish tobacco.

Tobacco produced in the New World other than in United States

The government of Canada has given a lot of attention to experiments in connection with the growth of tobacco in the Dominion, but only with indifferent success. The leaf is raised principally from Virginian seed, but is large and coarse and is only fit for inferior plug and snuff making.

Cuban Tobacco. The tobacco raised in the Island of Cuba is the most celebrated in the world for cigar making. The leaf is of a rich, brown color; narrow and small in size, varying from 8 to 18 inches in length. Its richness of flavor and the peculiar aroma are its chief characteristics. Cuba produces annually about 300,000 to 500,000 bales of tobacco varying in weight from 80 to 150 lbs. per bale, nearly one-half of which is exported to the United States alone.

The importation of Cuban leaf into the United States over a series of years is shown below:

Cuban leaf imports into the U. S. (lbs.)

1855-1860	==	7,014,485
1871-1875	==	8,985,465
1886-1890	==	15,532,075
1896-1900	==	10,811,173
1901-1905	==	24,048,837
Year 1914	==	26,617,545

The value in 1900 was $ 8,478,251

The value in 1905 was $13,348,000

The Province of Pinar del Rio produces about 70 per cent of the entire Cuban crop. In this is the District of Vuelto Abajo which is celebrated the world over for the very finest cigar tobacco. The District of Habana or Havana produces about 13 per cent and Santa Clara about 13 per cent. The Cubans themselves favor the dark "Maduro" fully ripened leaves. At present a good deal of Cuban cigar leaf is grown under shade with the result that although when fully mature they are light in color, they are rich in flavor.

The value of the cigar leaf imported by the U. S. from Cuba averages at present about 14 or 15 million dollars annually.

Porto Rican leaf possesses many of the qualities of good Havana leaf, and like the latter is used in cigar manufacture. The annual production is about 120,000 bales. The U. S. imports from 4 to 5 million lbs. annually. Further particulars regarding Cuban and Porto Rican leaf will be given in the chapters concerning cigars.

Mexico produces a tobacco, large as to leaf, dark in color, with heavy body and coarse veins. The tobacco is very strong in flavor. The best grades approach the Cuban tobacco in quality and are imported and used as substitutes for it. The U. S. importation is small. The annual production is about 34 million lbs. The best quality is produced in the neighborhood of Vera Cruz, and only a small portion is exported, principally to Cuba.

Brazilian tobacco leaf is brown in color, medium in size, and medium in body. It possesses fair qualities as a cigar tobacco, for which purpose it is generally used in South America, which is its principal market.

East Indian and Philippine Tobacco

The Dutch East Indies (Sumatra and the adjacent islands) produce yearly about 180 million lbs. of tobacco, all of which is used in the cigar business. Of this the United States takes about from 30,000 to 40,000 bales of Sumatran leaf, about 5½ million lbs. About 2 lbs. of this leaf wraps 1,000 cigars.

The Philippine Islands produce from 50 to 100 million lbs., of tobacco annually. The crop for 1913 was 101,544,736 lbs. The imports into the United States are principally as manufactured cigars by special arrangements which will be referred to later on in the chapter on cigars.

CHAPTER IV: PRODUCTION OF TOBACCO IN THE UNITED STATES

Total production. Amount produced by the different States. Varieties raised. Description of the different varieties.

The amount of tobacco leaf raised annually in the United States varies from 700 million lbs. to 1,000 million lbs. Thus, according to the Government Statistical Reports, the production in 1909 was 1,055,764,806 lbs., being an unusually high figure. The production in 1913 was 953,734,000 lbs. and in 1914; 1,034,679,000 lbs. The average crop may be taken as about 800 million lbs., about half of which is exported as leaf, and the other half manufactured in the U. S. into cigars, smoking and chewing tobaccos, etc., and consumed in the U. S.

To produce this immense crop over one million acres of rich, fertile land is under culture, the actual government figures for 1913 being 1,216,000 acres, and for 1914, 1,224,000, and the value of the raw crop is from 80 to 100 million dollars, which works out to an average value of from 10 to 12 cents per lb. The cost of producing the best grades of cigar leaf in the Eastern States is from 8 to 10 cents per lb.; in Wisconsin from 5 to 10 cents. The price paid to the growers is from 5 to 15 cents, except for the highest grades (cigar wrapper leaf) for which special prices, up to 40 or 50 cents, may be paid. Smoking and chewing leaf of average grade fetches from 6 to 7 cents per lb.

From these figures it will be seen that the agricultural industry of tobacco growing is a most important one, and it is constantly increasing both in the quantity produced and in value. About 45 of the states in the Union are engaged in tobacco culture, the principal states and the quantities produced being as follows (for 1914):

Kentucky	364	million lbs.
North Carolina	172	" "
Virginia	114	" "
Tennessee	63	" "

Ohio	78	"	"
Wisconsin	54	"	"
Pennsylvania	48	"	"
Connecticut	35	"	"
South Carolina	36	"	"
Maryland	17	"	"
Indiana	12	"	"
Massachusetts	11	"	"
Other states	30	"	"
Total	**1034**	**Million Pounds**	

Virginia was, until recently, the premier tobacco state. Tobacco was first raised in Virginia about 1619 when the quantity produced was about 20,000 lbs. By 1753 the records show that over 50 million lbs. were raised annually, all of which was exported. At this time and until about the period of the Civil War, Europe was dependant more than now on America for her tobacco supply, as at present a considerable part of her needs is supplied by her own production. Tobacco was not grown in Kentucky till about 1785 and a little later in Tennessee and Ohio. The cigar leaf industry of the New England States did not come into activity till about 1830. Cigar leaf was raised in Florida about the same time but was discontinued and was not resumed till fifty years later.

Virginia, Maryland and Tennessee have shown a declining annual production since the Civil War. Thus Virginia in 1860 produced nearly 30 percent of the total US crop, whereas at present it produces about 12 percent only. The causes which have contributed to the decline in tobacco culture in the Southern States are the loss of slave labor as well as the loss of capital during the war; more particularly it is due to the impoverishing of the soil without adequate fertilization. Thus with superior fertilization and intensive methods, Massachusetts and Connecticut give 1,750 lbs. to the acre, as against 870 and 580 lbs. for Kentucky and Tennessee. In Massachusetts and Connecticut the cost for fertilizer per farm is $227 as against $17 and $4 respectively in Tennessee and Kentucky. Moreover, the Northern farms are smaller than the Southern.

Varieties of Tobacco raised

The varieties of tobacco raised are mainly of the native American species; but in some states (in Florida particularly) plants are raised from imported Cuban and Sumatran seed, in an endeavor to produce cigar leaf equal in quality to the leaf now imported from these places which commands a high price in the trade. The raising of cigar leaf tobacco from foreign seed began in Florida about 1902; and, although on the whole, the cultivation has been very successful, yet it cannot be said that the hoped for results have been fully realized. It was claimed for the Florida grown Sumatran leaf that in many ways it surpassed the native Sumatran leaf. Certainly the experimental samples of this Florida leaf exhibited by the U. S. at the Paris Exposition of 1900 were judged to be superior both in appearance and style and other matters. However, this superiority does not appear to have been upheld, for in the trade the native grown Sumatran leaf still holds its rank.

Similarly in the case of Florida grown Cuban leaf which at the same Exposition was voted as equal to the native. The native leaf, however, whether due to the soil or not, has a finer flavor and aroma, and the best grades of native grown Cuban tobacco still hold the palm as the premier cigar tobacco of the world.

The leaf raised in Connecticut, Pennsylvania, Ohio, Wisconsin, Florida, Massachusetts, and New York State, is generally used for the cigar trade (see the chapters on cigars). Ohio and Florida (Cuban seed) leaf mostly used as cigar fillers; Connecticut and Florida (Sumatran seed), Pennsylvania and New York leaf mostly as wrapper leaf, the inferior leaves being used as fillers. Wisconsin leaf is used principally as cigar binder leaf. The total amount of cigar tobacco raised is roughly about one-fifth of the entire tobacco crop.

The southern states produce the bulk of the export dark, heavy leaf. West Kentucky and Tennessee particularly, as well as Virginia, the Carolinas and Maryland, export considerable quantities. This tobacco is fire-cured. For the domestic trade, however, (pipe-smoking, chewing and cigarettes) the tobacco grown in these states is flue-cured, the principal product being of a bright yellow color, characteristic of this region.

This "yellow tobacco belt" extends from the coast across to the North Carolina Mountains, through Tennessee and South Carolina, Southern Virginia, Southern Ohio, a few parts of Kentucky, some of Eastern Missouri and Arkansas. The best soils are those which are of a light sandy or sandy clay nature and they need not be deep or rich. In this region the very finest pipe-smoking tobaccos are raised. Whilst the U. S. has not been able to produce a cigar wrapper tobacco equal in quality to the Cuban or Sumatran, in pipe-smoking and cigarette tobaccos she stands without a rival.

There are about 100 different varieties of tobacco grown in the U. S., many of these being approximately the same and are synonymous. Subvarieties are easily obtained by gene crossing. Cross-fertilization easily takes place where different strains are produced in the same locality. On this account when it is desired to keep a variety pure, care must be exerted to see that seed is collected from pure strains. On the other hand, the ease of producing new varieties gives opportunity to the various State Agricultural Experimental Stations to try out new strains for desirable qualities. The enumeration of the differences between the various varieties would be tiresome for the reader, yet it will be well for the user of tobacco to know some of these varieties, their characteristics and other particulars concerning them. These are given here:

Leading Varieties of American Tobaccos

Burley. The variety known as White Burley has a long broad leaf, whitish in appearance when growing. The points of the leaf hang down towards the ground when growing, often even touching the ground. The leaf is thin in texture, has a mild flavor, low nicotine content and good absorbing qualities. It is one of the most popular tobaccos in the U. S. and is used for pipe-smoking and chewing tobaccos, snuff and cigarettes. It cures to a bright yellow brown color.

There is a variety known as Red Burley which has a thin leaf narrowing from center to top. The leaves are of a characteristic cinnamon color and are more elastic than those of White Burley. Burley tobacco is raised principally in Ohio, Kentucky, Virginia, Maryland, Missouri and Indiana.

Connecticut Seedleaf. Large, strong leaves, thin and elastic, silky in texture, small fibers, sweetish taste and light in color.

Used in the cigar trade as fillers and wrappers and grown in New England, Pennsylvania, Ohio, and to a smaller extent in Wisconsin, Minnesota, Indiana, Illinois and Florida.

Connecticut Broadleaf. A modification of the above, the leaves being broader in proportion to their length. They are up to 35 inches long and 22 inches wide. Largely used in the cigar trade as filler and wrappers. Both the Connecticut Seedleaf and Broadleaf are superior to the imported Sumatran leaf in flavor and aroma, but are inferior in elasticity and covering qualities. Grown principally in Connecticut and New York States.

Orinoco. There are 3 varieties of this name: (1) Short Orinoco. Broad leaf, upright growth and open habit, light colored, much ruffled. Grown in Virginia and Missouri. (2) Big Orinoco. Short, broad leaf. Grown in Virginia, Missouri, North Carolina, Tennessee and West Virginia. (3) Yellow Orinoco. Long, narrow, tapering leaf with fine texture. The sweetest variety grown. Grown in Virginia, Maryland, North Carolina, Tennessee, West Virginia and Missouri. Orinoco tobacco leaf is used largely for plug and smoking tobaccos and for the export trade.

Virginian. Sun and air-cured tobacco. Leaf is medium in size. Very bright brown color. Is rich in gums and oils which makes it sweet and fragrant and gives it a pleasant taste. Hence it is a favorite chewing tobacco.

Pryor. There are several varieties under this name: (1) Medley or White Pryor has a very broad leaf with silky texture and tough fiber. (2) Blue Pryor. Large, long fine leaf and good color. (3) Silky Pryor. A long sharp-pointed leaf; grows thin on the stalk; very tough and pliant. (4) Yellow Pryor. Heavy, wide leaf, fine bright color, tough and weighs well.

Pryor is used principally for the export trade and to some extent also in the home trade both for cigar and plug and smoking tobaccos. It is grown generally throughout Virginia, North Carolina, Kentucky, Tennessee, Missouri and Indiana, the White variety being extensively grown in Virginia.

Little Dutch. A very favorite pipe-smoking tobacco. It has a small nicotine content (less than 1%). The leaf is small; narrow, thick and short; dark brown in color, glossy surface and sweet in taste. It is grown extensively in the Miami Valley of Ohio.

Sumatra Seed. Grown principally in Florida from imported Sumatran seed. The leaf is light in weight and color, not long compared with other seedleaf varieties. Very narrow and with fine ribs. Used in cigar trade and grown extensively also in the New England states.

Cuban Seed. This has the usual qualities of Cuban tobacco but with inferior fragrance and aroma to the native grown. Principally raised in Pennsylvania, New York, Wisconsin, Connecticut and Florida for the cigar trade.

Perique. A special variety of tobacco grown only in a small area of Louisiana. The leaf is medium in size, has a fine fiber with small stems. Tough, gummy and glossy. It is grown in a deep, rich soil and grows very rapidly. Its special characteristics are acquired in the curing, which is a special process peculiar to itself, and which will be described in the chapter on Manufactured Tobaccos.

REFERENCES

Yearbooks of the United States Department of Agriculture. 1914 and previous.

Hoagland, I. G. *The Tobacco Industry.* In Quarterly of the National Fire Protection Association. 1907. Vol. I, Nos. 2 and 4.

Jacobstein, M. *The Tobacco Industry in the United States.* New York, 1907.

Billings, E. R. *Tobacco; its history, varieties, culture, manufacture and commerce.* Hartford Conn., 1875.

CHAPTER V: THE CHEMICAL COMPOSITION OF THE TOBACCO PLANT

Organic and inorganic matters contained in Tobacco and the parts they play. Analysis of various Tobaccos. Nicotine.

THE CHEMICAL COMPOSITION OF THE TOBACCO PLANT

The tobacco plant when subjected to chemical analysis is found to contain all or most of the following substances:

Mineral Bases: Potash, Lime, Magnesia, Oxides of Iron and Manganese, Ammonia, Silica.

Mineral Acids: Nitric, Hydrochloric, Sulphuric and Phosphoric.

Organic Base: Nicotine.

Organic Acids: Malic, Citric, Acetic, Oxalic, Pectic and Ulmic.

Other Organic Substances: Nicotianin, Green and Yellow Resin, Wax and Fat, Nitrogenous Substances and Cellulose.

The substances which differentiate tobacco from other plants and form its chief characteristics are **Nicotianin, Nicotine** and **Malic Acid.**

The percentage in which the important substances exist in tobacco is given below:

Nicotine : From 1 to 9%

Malic and Citric Acids: From 10 to 14%

Oxalic Acid: From 1 to 2%

Resins, Oils and Fats: From 4 to 6%

Pectic Acid: About 5%

Cellulose: From 7 to 8%

Albumenoids: About 25%

Ash: From 12 to 30%

When tobacco is burned, chemical changes occur; the organic and other compounds are decomposed. The volatile matters pass off in the smoke if the combustion is complete, and the mineral ash remains. In ordinary pipe or other tobacco smoking, however, the combustion is not complete and many decomposition products remain with the mineral ash.

In tobacco smoke the following can usually be found: Furfurol, Marsh Gas, Hydrogen Sulphide, Hydrogen Cyanide, Organic Acids, Phenols, Empyreumatic Oils, Pyridine, Picoline Series and possibly some Nicotine.

The ash left after complete combustion is important, as much of the smoking qualities of the tobacco depends on its constituents. An average sample gives the following analysis (in 100 parts):

Average mineral contents of tobacco ash:

Potash: 27%

Soda: 3%

Lime: 40%

Magnesia: 9%

Sodium Chloride: 9%

Sulphuric Acid: 3%

Silica: 5%

Lime Phosphate: 4%

Remarks on Some of the Substances Found in Tobacco

Nicotine

Of all the substances found in tobacco, nicotine is the most important. Nicotine in the pure state is a colorless liquid having a specific gravity of 1.027. It is an organic base having the chemical formula $C_{10}H_{14}N_2$. It is extremely acidic and burning to the taste, and is a virulent poison. It easily volatilizes; is inflammable, and is soluble in water, alcohol, ether and some fixed oils. Nicotine has the characteristic peculiar odor of tobacco.

The amount of nicotine in tobacco is said to depend on the nature of the soil in which it is grown; rich, heavy soils and strong nitrogenous manuring favor the production of a large nicotine content; and light, sandy soils the opposite.

THE BIOSYNTHESIS OF NICOTINE

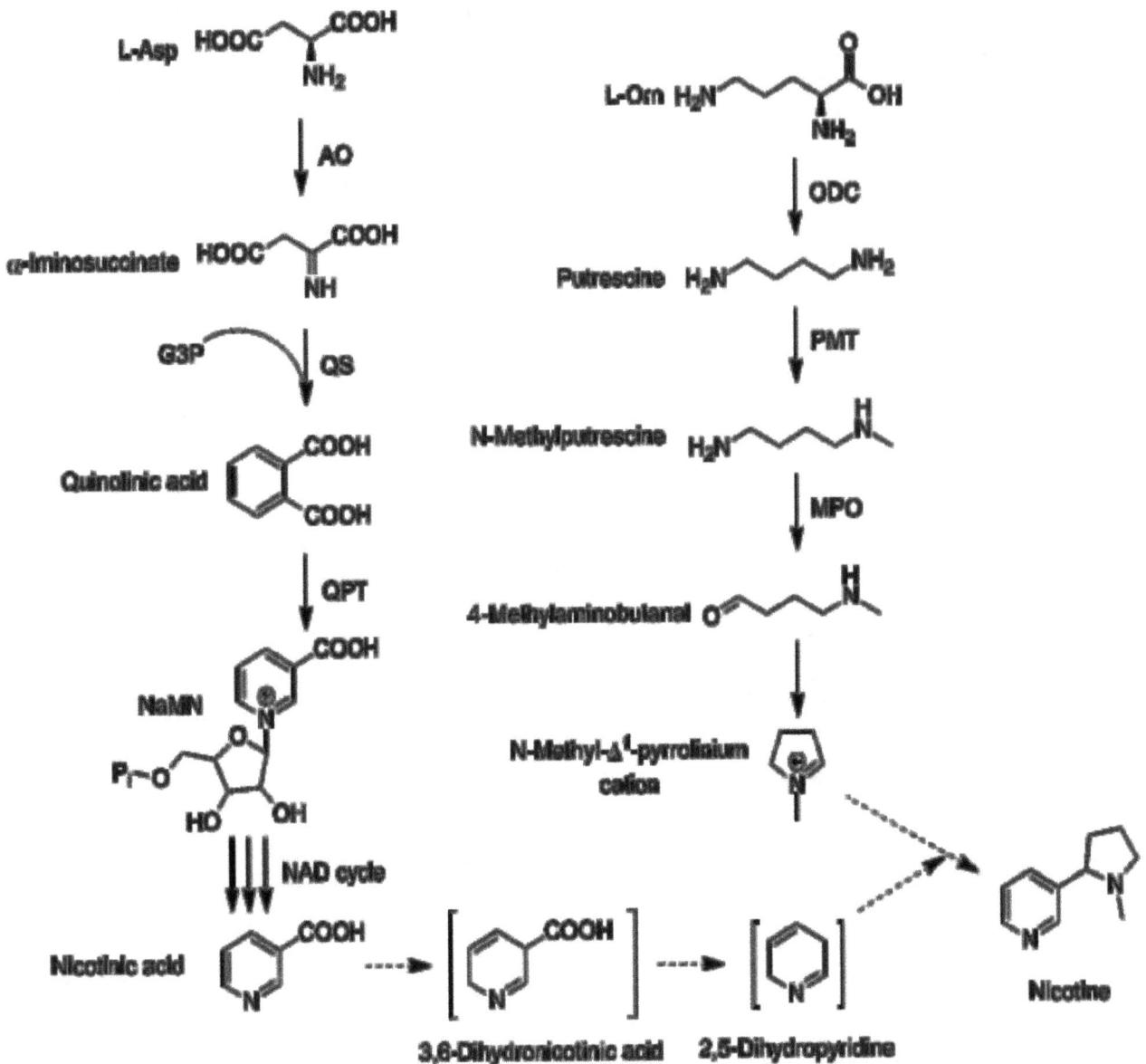

What tobacco looks like on paper. The molecular breakdown of nicotine as shown above has served as the key to understanding exactly how nicotine effects our bodies when consumed.

Scientists working outside of the tobacco industry use this very same chart to develop pharmaceutical alternatives to cigarette smoking such as Nicorette, lozenges and insufflated inhalants. More infamously, Philip Morris used this blueprint to develop more potent strains of nicotine in their cigarette tobacco specifically to keep the smoker "hooked" on their product. The first cigarette brand to utilize the experimental "super nicotine" was Marlboro, which, coincidentally or not, became the best selling filtered cigarette of all time.

Moreover the nicotine content depends on the age and development of the plant. An investigation by Chuard and Mellet showed nicotine contents of leaves:

In young plants 7 weeks old contained   .0324%

In plants 10 weeks old contained   .0447%

In plants 13 weeks old contained   .4989%

In plants 19 weeks old contained   .9202%

The longer the plant is permitted to grow the larger will be its nicotine content. Schlössing has made a similar investigation and found that in the same plant the nicotine content varies from 0.79% when young to 4.32% when fully matured. Most nicotine is found in the ribs and veins.

H. B. Cox (American Druggist V. 24, 1894, p. 95) investigated the nicotine contents of various manufactured tobaccos. These were not "proprietary tobaccos" but samples obtained from different sources at random. His results are given here:

Nicotine Contents of Different Tobaccos

Syrian Tobacco leaf (a)	.612%
American Chewing Leaf	.935%
Syrian Tobacco Leaf (b)	1.093%
Chinese Tobacco Leaf	1.902%
Turkish Coarse Cut	2.500%
Golden Virginia (whole strips)	2.501%
Gold Flake Virginia	2.501%
Navy Cut (light)	2.530%
Light Kentuckian	2.733%
Navy Cut (dark)	3.64 %
Best "Bird's Eye"	3.931%
Cut Cavendish (a)	4.212%
Best Shag (a)	4.907%
Cut Cavandish (b)	4.970%
Best Shag (b)	5.00 %
Algerian Tobacco (a)	8.813%
French Grown Tobacco	8.711%
Algerian Tobacco (b)	8.90 %

The average of a number of samples of Syrian tobacco showed 1 to 2% nicotine, Manila and Havana 1 to 3%, Virginia and Kentucky from 2 to 7%, and French tobaccos about 9%.

Most of the nicotine in tobacco becomes volatilized and decomposed during combustion; a small part, however, may form a solution with the water which is also one of the combustion products. One of the decomposition products of nicotine is Pyridine.

Pyridine is usually found in tobacco smoke. When condensed it is a colorless non-oily liquid and is considerably less toxic than nicotine.

Reference will be made later on to the effects of nicotine and pyridine on the human system.

Potash is important as on its amount depends the burning qualities of the tobacco. It is sometimes present in the ash to the extent of 30%, being converted into potassium carbonate by burning. Not only for free burning is the potash valuable, but also for the better volatilization of the nicotine and other substances. The more perfect the combustion, the fewer deleterious compounds are formed.

Chlorides, if present, retard the burning of the tobacco, and hence a tobacco which contains a high percentage of chloride, even if it is rich in potash salts, is a poor burning tobacco and therefore faulty. While it is important that the burning should be free and the volatilization as perfect as possible, yet the smoker does not want his tobacco to burn too rapidly. To meet this some manufacturers prepare "slow burning" tobaccos generally by the addition of some chemical which checks the potash.

The aroma and flavor of the tobacco depend to a great extent on the waxes, resins and oils, as well as on certain of the organic acids.

REFERENCES

U. S. Dispensatory. 1907 (19th Edition).

Kissling. *The Chemistry of Tobacco.* Scientific American (Supp.) 1905, Vol. 60, No. 1560.

Chuard & Mellett. *Variation de Nicotine dans les differents organes de la plante de Tabac.* Comp. Rend. Acad. d. Sc. (Paris) 1912. Vol. 155, p. 293.

Pezzolato, A. *Conferenza Sulla Chimica applicato alla technologia del Tabacco.* (Rome. 1903.)

Wolf, Jacob. *Der Tabak und die Tabak fabrikate.* Chapter III. Leipzig, 1912.

Schlossing. *Sur la production de la nicotine par la culture du Tabac.* Compt. Rend. Acad. d. Sc. (Paris), 1910. Vol. 151, p. 23.

CHAPTER VI: THE CURING OF TOBACCO LEAF

Objects of curing. Methods.

THE CURING OF TOBACCO LEAF

The "curing" of tobacco leaf is the process of drying out which has for its object the following specific actions:

(1) The expelling of the sap and superfluous moisture.

(2) The completion of the "yellowing" process and the fixing of the desired color.

(3) The preservation of the juices, etc., which give the characteristic flavor and aroma.

(4) To give the necessary toughness and suppleness to the leaf.

The first part of the curing is done by the grower in curing sheds on the farm immediately after the cutting of the crop; the final part, or the fermentation part is usually done by the leaf dealer or manufacturer in special buildings called leaf-houses.

There are three methods of curing in use by the growers, i. e., sun curing, air curing, and artificial heat curing. In the case of the tobacco known as Perique the curing process is more or less peculiar to itself. "Sun" and "air" curing are much slower processes than the curing by artificial heat.

All cigar leaf tobacco is sun-cured; as a general rule pipe smoking and chewing tobacco are cured by artificial heat.

For the purpose of drying and curing by artificial heat, the leaf is hung up in specially constructed curing houses or sheds. It is found that after the exposure to the sun for the first process of "yellowing" tobacco leaf still contains 1 lb.

of water approximately in each plant. The first part of the process of curing consists in drawing off this superfluous moisture. Dry heat is applied at a temperature of 90° F. to 120° F. for about 16 to 30 hours to effect this. A further exposure of about 48 hours at a temperature of 125° or so is necessary to complete the curing, and fix the color.

The stems and stalks being thicker take a longer time and generally require 9 to 10 hours further exposure and a temperature which may range as high as 175° F. before they are fully cured, the temperature being graded hourly until the maximum necessary is reached.

The process of curing varies considerably in different states. Some growers prefer to put the tobacco into the sheds immediately after cutting, and allow very little exposure in the fields. The temperature is usually kept steady at about 90° F. Again the process is different according to the quality of tobacco required.

For the heavy type of leaf which is intended for the export trade, the curing in the sheds is done by an open fire, the fuel being usually hardwood logs. The smoky, creosotic flavor is absorbed by the leaf, and, although this flavor is not relished by the smokers of the U. S., it is much liked in Europe. The curing in such cases may last for 4 or even 5 days. The tobacco is suspended on poles by the stalks and the fires are built on the floor immediately under them so that the carbonaceous products are easily absorbed by the open pores of the leaf.

The chewing and pipe smoking tobacco, as well as cigarette tobaccos including all the bright yellow tobaccos used in the U. S. are usually cured by Flue curing. In this case the heat comes from pipes which run around the curing houses and are fed from a furnace in an adjoining chamber or in a cellar. The temperature can be easily regulated. "Flue" curing is generally completed in about 4 days. "Flue" curing does not clog up the pores of the leaf which therefore remain more absorbent than in the open fire cured tobacco. This is an important matter for the manufacturers because the flue cured leaf will absorb twice as much of the flavoring sauces (which are added to certain kinds of tobacco) than tobacco leaf cured by open fires.

Air exposure of 6 to 8 weeks (sometimes extended to 3 or 4 months) is necessary when tobacco is cured by exposure to the sun and air. It is claimed, however, that this method of curing preserves far better the natural flavor of the leaf; and, where flavor and aroma are highly important, this method is always preferred. Hence all cigar leaf tobaccos are cured by exposure to natural sunlight and not by artificial heat.

"Air" curing as distinct from sun curing is generally done in open sheds which are thoroughly ventilated and kept as far as possible at a temperature of about 75° F. The leaf is usually allowed to cure while attached to the stalk, but Florida curers generally prefer to strip the leaf and treat it separately. The finer classes of pipe smoking tobaccos are air cured.

After the curing is completed the color of the leaf is usually fixed. Generally speaking, the riper the leaf the lighter will be its color when cured. Thus the bottom leaves of the plant will be lighter in color than the upper leaves because they are more mature. (For references see end of Chapter VIII.)

CHAPTER VII: THE MARKETING AND SALE OF TOBACCO LEAF

Methods of disposal by the grower. The Warehouse system. Direct purchase. Principal markets in the United States. Prices.

THE MARKETING AND SALE OF TOBACCO LEAF

When the tobacco leaf is fully cured it is at once prepared for the market. The first step is the planters' classification of the leaf. In the case of pipe smoking and chewing tobacco the planter collects all the imperfect, injured leaves, or those inferior from any cause, and ties them in bundles. These are the planters lugs. All other grades are leaf. Slightly injured leaves are classed as low-leaf or seconds. The others are classed medium, good, fine and selected leaf, according to grade, color, quality, etc.

In the case of cigar leaf tobacco a similar classification is made, more care being taken owing to the very great difference in price between the better and poorer qualities. This difference may be as much as .20 in the lb., the finer and more suitable leaf being eagerly sought for.

Pipe smoking and chewing tobacco leaf is usually packed in hogsheads or cases each weighing from 1,000 to 1,400 lbs. The operation of packing the leaf is called "prizing." Cigar leaf is usually put up in "hands." A "hand" consists of from 25 to 75 leaves tied together. Four hands tied together make a "carrot" and 80 carrots go to the bale, but the size of the bale varies considerably. The tobacco is then ready for the buyer.

There are two systems of disposing of the planters' product: (1) direct purchase by the manufacturer or by a middleman from the grower; and (2) what is known as the warehouse system. In the southern states the warehouse system prevails. Every important tobacco section in the south has its public warehouse which is under the control and supervision of state law. Many of these warehouses are long established, that at Richmond, Va., dating as far back as 1730, and those at Louisville and Clarksville about 1839.

On appointed days the planter brings his leaf to the warehouse. Here it is entered as "loose leaf" or "inspected leaf." In the case of loose leaf, the tobacco is open to the inspection of prospective buyers, who examine it and afterwards bid on it. In the case of "inspected leaf" the warehouse officials first examine the consignments, grade them and mark them according to their judgment, taking samples. The samples are open to buyers' inspection and form the basis of sale. Tobacco auctions are regularly held when the buyers assemble and bid on the "loose leaf" and "inspected" lots. Prices of the various grades are fixed and sales take place at the day's price.

The principal tobacco markets are:

For Kentucky and Tennessee—At Louisville, Clarksville and Cincinnati.

For Maryland and Ohio—At Baltimore.

For North Carolina—At Durham and Winston.

For Virginia—At Richmond.

The warehouse system has the great advantage that the proceedings are open and the prices are recorded and published. Hence growers can know how the market fluctuates and judge the best time for sale. This is not the case when the sale is private between the buyer and seller as is customary in the eastern and northern states. Here the price actually received by the grower is often different from that given out as paid.

The price of tobacco leaf has had many vicissitudes during the past 25 years, the price often having reached so low a point as to discourage producers. Thus at Winston, NC, the price has gradually fallen from 12.3 cents per lb. in 1889 to 6.3 cents in 1896. In the same period Burley leaf at Louisville and Cincinnati fell from 10c cents to 7½ cents. Prices similarly dropped in other centers. The price of cigar leaf has latterly increased. In 1900 prices ran from 6 to 15 cents; in 1905 from 8 to 17 cents. Many conditions at home and abroad affect the price, such as bad harvests or inferior grades of produce.

The tobacco trust has been very unjustly blamed by many for the falling price of tobacco. As a matter of fact and record, however, the concentration of buying power by eliminating the middleman and the small dealers has not only placed the grower in a better position by giving him a better price, as recent records show, but it has benefited the consumer also who can obtain the superior grades at a lower price. It is the middleman's profit that has been cut.

Moreover, the concentrated buying power of the large interests here has been an effective force in keeping up tobacco leaf prices against the foreign buyers. It must be remembered that about half of our crop is exported. The buyers of this portion, who are principally the agents of foreign governments (in the cases where tobacco is a government monopoly as in France, Italy, etc.) assemble at the auctions and bid in the usual way. As this competition is very limited there is always an opportunity for such buyers to agree among themselves as to the limit of prices. This has been one of the important factors which has kept the prices of tobacco leaf down. The concentration of American buying power has, however, been a formidable check on it, the prices received by the growers being now fair and reasonable, and such as are the result of a healthy market, where the factors of supply and demand have their full share of effect.

The government statistics show that for 1914 the prices of leaf varied from 5.5 cents to 20 cents for common to good varieties. (For references see end of Chapter VIII.)

CHAPTER VIII: REHANDLING AND FERMENTATION OF TOBACCO LEAF PRIOR TO MANUFACTURE

Selection of leaf. Treatment and Blending. Objects and methods of Fermentation. Action of microbes.

REHANDLING AND FERMENTATION OF TOBACCO LEAF PRIOR TO MANUFACTURE

We have seen how the tobacco passes from the grower to the manufacturer or leaf dealer. Before it is fitted, however, for manufacture into cigars or other finished products the leaf must go through many processes, the most important of which is fermentation. These processes, which are usually known as rehandling, are carried out in special buildings which are called leaf houses and stemmeries. The procedures in different leaf houses may vary somewhat, but the general principles and objects in view are the same in all. Moreover, the treatment is different, according to the ulterior disposition of the leaf, i. e. whether intended for cigars, pipe smoking or other product. The general treatment as carried out in large establishments is about as follows:

The leaf as soon as it is received whether in casks, cases, bales, or otherwise is opened up and inspected in the casing room. Large concerns which manufacture or deal in cigar and other kinds of leaf, sort out the different kinds suitable for each class of product, i.e. wrappers, fillers, binders, cigarette leaf, plug leaf, etc.

These are distributed to either special houses or departments. The tobacco leaf when first received is usually dry and brittle. The bundles are carefully opened up and the leaves loosened and spread out on large trucks where they are sprayed with water. When the leaf has soaked the water and is pliable it undergoes a sorting which is done by selecting leaves from different cases or even bundles of leaves and in a general way arranging them so that each truckfull represents a blend of the different kinds of leaf which are suitable for the purpose in view. These sorted packages are then roughly fastened together and after being again sprinkled thoroughly are sent to the "sweating" room to undergo fermentation which may last several weeks. The temperature of this room must be carefully regulated and is usually kept at about 90° F.

The selection and blending of the different kinds of leaf is most important. It requires accurate and expert knowledge in choosing leaves and kinds possessing different strengths and other qualities and in combining them in such proportions that the final effect of the blend gives just what is required.

It is particularly in this expert treatment of the leaf before manufacture that the greatest advance has been made in the tobacco industry. The smoker has the advantage and satisfaction of knowing that not only does he get the benefit of improved scientific knowledge and sanitary conditions by which anything that might be harmful or undesirable is removed, but that handling the leaf in large quantities effects great economics and procures for him the benefit of choicest selected grades at a reduced cost.

It may be said here incidentally that leaves of the very best tobaccos which are defective merely in size, or color, etc., are put through exactly the same processes as the choicer quality leaves, and are used in the manufacture of the popular priced machine-made "little cigars" and "cheroots."

It will be necessary now to digress for a short time and consider what happens during the process of fermentation.

Fermentation of Tobacco

The fermenting of tobacco leaf has for its principal objects, (1) the removal of acrid matters, (2) the fixing of the color, and (3) the production of flavor. Fermentation can

FERMENTATION OF CIGAR TOBACCO

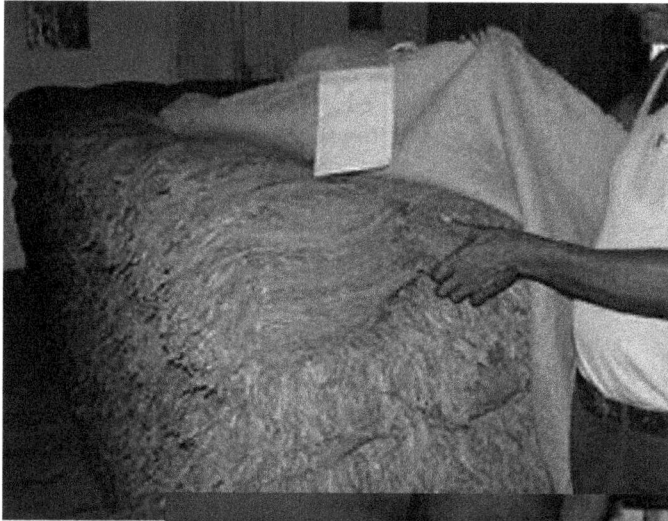

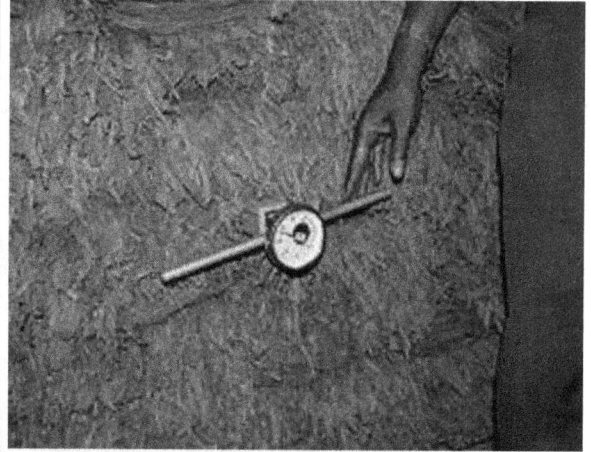

Perhaps the most important part of the curing process is the fermentation stage. Cuban cigar makers are masters of the art, still using the same barrels and casks that date to the late 1800s.

If the tobacco is fermented too rapidly, the taste of the cigar is raw and bitter. If left to ferment too long, the tobacco rots and molds over, making the leaf unsmokable. Either error can damage an entire season's worth of tobacco crop. [Photos courtesy of Cuba Junkie.com].

only take place under suitable conditions of heat and moisture, and is essentially a chemical process during which certain organic compounds stored in the plant are split up and others formed.

A certain amount of fermentation takes place in the curing houses during the "yellowing" of the leaf after it has been harvested, but as we have seen the main process of fermentation does not occur until it is "rehandled" by the manufacturers.

The general opinion held at present as the result of investigation is that the transformations which are effected in the leaf are purely the result of chemical processes. As the plant slowly dies and decomposes special ferments are produced. These ferments set up an oxidization process which splits up the complex organic compounds which still exist in the leaf cells. The starch in the plant is changed into sugar which is slowly consumed.

There is a decrease in the fats and gummy substances, also in nicotine and nitrogenous compounds, and there is a formation of certain organic acids such as malic, citric and oxalic which are essential in the production of flavor. Briefly it may be said that the process is an attempt by the plant to prolong its existence by feeding on its own substance, by drawing on its own reserves and on its own structure for the food which its cells no longer receive through the natural growing process. When the struggle is over the "fermentation" is complete.

The necessity for maturing tobacco has long been known but the exact nature of the changes that take place during the process were not understood. Since the discoveries of Louis Pasteur regarding the part played by bacteria in general fermentative processes it has been generally claimed by bacteriologists that the changes wrought in the leaf and the production of flavor are solely the work of bacteria. Although this view has not been proved, it has never been fully disproved, and there appears to be no doubt that the microbes known to exist in the leaf during the fermentation process play an important part in the process. Fermentation can only take place as stated under suitable conditions of heat and moisture and these are the conditions which favor the development of microbes and enable them to work. The results obtained are probably partially due to chemical action and partly to bacterial action, the two being complementary to each other.

In 1899 Suchsland, a German scientist, startled the tobacco world by asserting that the flavor of tobacco was in no way due to the effects of the soil and climate where it was grown, but was solely due to microbic action, and that the specific flavor and aroma of any given tobacco could be artificially produced by the cultivation of selected bacteria and allowing the tobacco to cure and ferment under their action. He conducted a series of experimental investigations in which he searched for and isolated the specific microbes found in the best West Indian tobacco. From these he made artificial cultures and introduced them into heaps of inferior, coarse German tobacco which was undergoing curing.

His results were such that the smoking quality of the leaf was entirely changed. It could scarcely be distinguished from the best Cuban tobacco and experts and connoisseurs failed to identify the product as German tobacco. A company was formed to exploit the new ideas commercially, but it does not appear to have met with success. Other investigations failed to obtain Suchsland's results and extensive investigation in the Agricultural Experimental Station in the United States have not up to now produced any results confirmatory of the theory.

We can now proceed to follow the course of the tobacco in its peregrinations through the leaf house.

On their return from the first fermentation the bundles go to the picking department. Leaves which are damaged or unsuitable in any way are here picked out and put aside to be used in the cheaper grades. The leaves are then subjected to a thorough cleaning to remove particles of sand, clay, etc., packed tightly in bundles and returned to the sweating department to undergo further fermentation and to allow for a thorough interchange of the aroma of the different blends. In due course the bundles pass to the stemming department for the removal of the midribs which usually form nearly one-third of the entire weight. The resulting half leaves are then arranged in piles of 50, each pile forming a "book."

From the stemming department the books pass to the drying room where any superfluous moisture is removed by hot air currents.

From the drying room the books pass to the ordering room where they undergo inspection for color, size, etc., and subjected to further treatment if necessary. Here they are finally packed in cases and stored for several months to allow perfect and uniform blending after which they are ready for shipment to the factory. Filler leaf for the finest cigars may stand in these cases for two or three years.

Leaf which is intended for chewing or pipe smoking is not subjected to so great an elaboration of processes as cigar leaf, as the matters of uniformity of color, and delicacy as well as individuality of aroma are not of such great importance. Usually such tobacco leaf is fermented in bulk, and the removal of the stems is done before the principal fermentation.

After the preliminary selection of varieties, sorting, stemming and cleaning, the leaf is dipped into large vats containing flavors; and after drying are subjected to steaming. They are then packed away in bulk in the sweating department where they slowly ferment until required for use. These "bulks" or stacks may contain many tons of leaf. They require constant turning over, etc. Indeed it may be said that every step in these processes requires constant care. Temperature, moisture, length of exposure, etc., must all be carefully seen to. Otherwise the tobacco will spoil.

In the case of tobacco leaf intended for export trade rehandling consists mainly of stemming and removal of moisture. This is done before shipment in order to reduce the weight as customs duty is levied in accordance with the weight of the imported packages in the countries importing.

REFERENCES

U. S. Depart. of Agric. Farmers' Bulletins 6 and 60.

Laureut, L. *Le Tabac, sa culture et sa preparation, production et consommation.* Paris, 1900.

Bouant, E. *Le Tabac; culture et industrie.* Paris, 1901.

Boekhout und de Vries. *Uber Tabacfermentation.* "Centralbl. f. Bakter," 1909. 2 Abteil. Vol. 24, p. 496.

Loew, O. *Sind Bakterien die Ursache der Tabakfermentation?* "Centralbl. f. Bakter," 1909. Vol. 6, p. 108.

Killebrew and Myrick. *Tobacco Leaf.* Part I. New York, 1897.

Suchsland, E. *Bobachtungen über die Selbsterwärmung des fermentierenden Tabaks. In "Festschrift 200-Jahr Jubel. d. Verein. Friedrichs Universit."* Halle-Wittenberg, 1894.

Wolf, Jakob. *Der Tabak und die Tabakfabrikate.* Chapter IV. Leipzig, 1912.

Hoagland, J. G. T*he Tobacco Industry.* In Quarterly of the Nat. Fire Protec. Assn., 1907. Vol. 1, Nos. 2 and 4.

Jacobstein, M. T*he Tobacco Industry in the U. S. Chapter II.* New York, 1907.

CHAPTER IX: MANUFACTURED PRODUCTS OF TOBACCO IN THE UNITED STATES

Statistics of production and consumption. Amount of capital invested, etc.

MANUFACTURED PRODUCTS OF TOBACCO.
GENERAL REMARKS

The importance and magnitude of the tobacco manufacturing industry in the United States will be best understood from a consideration of the following statistics taken from the latest available government records:

(For all Manufactured Products)

Cost of materials used (1905) $==$ \$126,000,000

(1909) $==$ 177,000,000

Value of the product (1905) $==$ 331,000,000

(1909) $==$ 417,000,000

No. of establishments (1905) $==$ 16,828

(1909) $==$ 15,822

No. of persons employed, more than one-third being women:

(1905) $==$ 160,000

(1909) $==$ 197,000

The figures are given in round numbers. The total capital invested in this industry is between \$300,000,000 and \$400,000,000.

There are more than one and a quarter millions acres in the U. S. under cultivation of tobacco which yields a crop at present approximating to 1,000 million lbs. of leaf annually.

The industry shows an absolutely increasing condition in every particular at each census. During the past 45 years the value of the product has increased more than \$300,000,000.

In addition to the trade in manufacturing in the U. S. there is the export trade principally in unmanufactured leaf. This amounts at present to about \$54,000,000 annually. The price of export leaf has been continuously increasing despite of the fact that the production of leaf abroad is increasing. Thus in 1886 the average export price of leaf from the U. S. was 8½ cents per lb. In 1914 it was more than 12 cents.

The following statement shows at a glance the marvelous increase in the tobacco industry:

Comparative Statement of Manufactured Tobacco in the USA (all products):

Capital invested/ Number of employees/ Value of product:

Year 1880	$ 39,000,000	86,000	$126,000,000
Year 1890	90,000,000	117,000	195,000,000
Year 1900	111,000,000	142,000	264,000,000
Year 1905	324,000,000	159,000	330,000,000
Year 1909	?	197,000	417,000,000

In addition to the number of persons employed in manufacturing we must take into account those employed (as well as the capital invested) in the agricultural and distributing ends. (The export manufacturing trade is not important, being only valued at about 3 million dollars annually.)

The value of the home manufactured products which in 1905 was shown at $330,000,000 is distributed as follows.

Cigars	$198,000,000
Cigarettes	16,000,000
Chewing and smoking tobaccos	109,000,000
Snuff	6,000,000
Other products	1,000,000
Total	$330,000,000

For the increase in the present value of the product these figures would be proportionately increased.

In the year 1913 the United States exported about 350 million lbs. of unmanufactured tobacco leaf, and in 1914, 449 million lbs. This was distributed as follows:

To G. Britain/Ireland	174	million lbs.	
To Canada	17	"	"
To France	55	"	"
To Germany	32	"	"
To Italy	45	"	"
To Netherlands	28	"	"
To Spain	17	"	"
To Japan	16	"	"
To China	11	"	"
To Belgium	11	"	"
All Other Countries	43	"	"
Total:	449	Million Pounds	

The largest export manufacturing trade was to Asia, the cigarettes exported there having a value of 2½ million dollars.

The consumption of manufacturing products of tobacco in the U. S. has increased continuously since 1863 when it was 1.6 lbs. per head to the present time when it is 5½ lbs. per head of the total population. This works out at about 16 lbs. per head for each male over 16 years. The consumption of tobacco in the U. S. is higher than in any other country and has increased more rapidly.

For the past 40 years the consumption per head in the US has increased 240%; in England 56%; in France 24%; in Germany 23%. From this fact different deductions might be made. It may be that the Americans smoke more because they are fonder of tobacco than Europeans; or because they get better and cheaper tobacco; or because they can better afford to buy tobacco. The greatest percentage of increase in the United States is in the consumption of cigars.

The manufactured products are classed as (1) cigars, (2) pipe smoking and chewing tobaccos, (3) cigarettes, (4) snuff. To each of these separate chapters will be devoted. (For references see Chapter XV.)

Come back next issue where we finish our reprint of Tobacco Leaves. *This second half of our reprint features specific chapters about pipes, cigars, snuff and chewing tobacco. Thanks for reading!*

WARNING: This product can cause mouth cancer.

Keep on Snuffin' in the Free World

How Anti-Tobacco Fascism is Threatening Everyone's Freedom

By Lew Snusman

Do no harm to others. This seems like a perfectly reasonable edict by which to live. A strong argument can be made that secondhand, and possibly even thirdhand smoke causes harm to others. Therefore, subjecting someone to smoke can be considered harmful if being exposed to it is something to which they are not agreeable. The Golden Rule applies here. Perhaps this was best said in Galatians 5:14, "For all law is fulfilled in one word, even this; Thou shalt love thy neighbor as thyself." Certainly this statement is open to debate, however to wish ill upon another human is evil even if, in your opinion, they are perpetrating illness upon themselves. One shall not subject another to smoke if they do not agree just as one shall not condemn one for smoking because they do not agree with the habit, so long as the harm is contained to those agreeable to the potential consequences. The snuff taker however, subjects no one to anything and yet is treated as if they are perpetrating harm upon others. In either case, that of the smoker or that of the snuff taker, forceful actions not only threaten the natural rights of the tobacco user; these actions threaten the rights and freedom of every individual.

How does one love thy neighbor as thyself? To start it begins with accepting that views of vice and virtue are nebulous at best and destructive to the fabric of humanity at worst. To the teetotaler a single drink after work could be considered detrimental to society and all who consume alcohol are responsible for all of humanity's ills. As the United States learned during the prohibition such insane views, when enacted into law, not only violate the liberty of others they result in widespread crime, violence, corruption and national insecurity. Morality cannot be defined or regulated and inane efforts to do so create only more of the things in which the original initiatives set out to counteract.

Users of tobacco have become subject to the same oppressive persecutions which have proven disastrous in the past, and they're not the only ones. Somehow all tobacco use has become part of a "public health issue" that is subject to excessive taxation, de facto prohibition (if not outright in the case of snus in the EU) and discriminatory practices against the user. The swine have found the trough and they feast upon the beleaguered tobacco user and others in an ever growing manner. Many would say that a tobacco tax is a tax upon the poor as many a tobacco user are working class or poorer. The problem is that the pigs must continue to binge and they will feast upon the freedoms of all if their gluttonous ways are left unchecked. If you don't believe this, you haven't looked around. Restriction and taxation on tobacco has opened the door to further restriction and taxation on other items. We need only to look to Czar Bloomberg in New York who has limited the amount of soda one can buy apparently to protect the soda drinker from themselves. Such an assault on freedom would have been laughable in the past, but then again so wouldn't tobacco restricted outdoor areas and First Amendment zones.

Tobacco was and is an easy scapegoat; it was a palatable way to get a large amount of the public comfortable with freedom robbing restrictions and taxation that actually eclipses the total price of the

ABORTION IS EVERY WOMAN'S RIGHT! IT'S HER BODY AND HER CHOICE!

NOW I'D LIKE TO UNVEIL MY NEW BILL TO BAN SODA, SALT, SUGAR, SMOKING, CAKE, CANDY, MEAT AND TOBACCO.

PROGRESSIVISM

Still EVIDENT

product. Government intervention on tobacco use has softened us up, desensitized us, to the ever growing nanny state. It is part of a slow process to continue to reduce freedoms, weaken the voice of the average citizen and grow government beyond a reasonable and sustainable level. When the government takes away the freedom of its citizens, it's theft, it's an act of aggression. I'd say that violates the Golden Rule. The worrisome thing is that many of us are either unaware that we are being stripped of our freedoms or we're too apathetic and lazy to do anything about it.

The thing about freedom that we must keep in mind is that it is not a la carte. You cannot take away one freedom to which you are opposed and expect that a freedom that is acceptable to you will be spared. Eventually each increment of freedom that is given away will add up to a total loss of individual liberty. Too often people want to tax or eliminate the things to which they're opposed regardless of how it encroaches on others rights, but cannot see how this will one day tax or eliminate something they support. This is the folly of democracy. Democracy teaches that individual rights are negotiable which is antithetical to the foundations of a free society. In a democracy the frothing masses can vote away the rights of others. If you can vote away the rights of tobacco users, you can vote away the rights of people of religion, people of color, people of foreign descent, workers, farmers and any other people who create the strong fabric of a free nation.

To protect your own freedom, you must stand with the tobacco taker. This does not mean that you must be exposed to a smoker's smoke, but you must support their right to engage in this habit. For the user of smokeless tobacco, you must stand by he or she with even more vigor for they do you no harm. The rights and the liberties of the tobacco user are linked to the rights and liberties of all, so the next time you see someone partake of snuff thank them for exercising their freedoms for in their act they are standing up for the rights of all individuals.

STE

STRANGE... BUT TRUE !

TOBACCO-RELATED ODDITIES AND ANECDOTES

COMPILED BY DAVID THIGPEN

Hot Hot Hot

A man in Wisconsin was treated for third degree burns in December, 2012 after trying to light a cigarette off of his stove burner.

Reynold McMartin stated that his lighter was out of fluid and he was unable to find any matches in his house, so he set the gas burner on his stove in order to light his cigarette.

As he leaned over to light his cigarette, the circle of flame unexpectedly flared up into an inferno, which burned off his moustache and eyebrows. His live-in boyfriend heard screams and after rushing in to the kitchen, saw McMartin sprawled out on the floor with a wet rag covering his face. When the boyfriend removed the rag, he was horrified to see the damage. "All of his facial hair was gone, and his eyebrows, and some of his hair [on his head]. He was barely conscious."

McMartin spent two weeks in the hospital before being released. Though he is scarred for life, he is expected to make a full recovery and has stated that he will possibly be looking into plastic surgery in the near future to heal his scars.

The Birth of Filtered Cigarettes

The first known filtered cigarette was invented in 1925 by Boris Aivas, an Hungarian Jew in what is now modern Slovakia.

Aivas was inspired to make filter tipped cigarettes one day as he was driving around town with his convertible top down. Unable to locate his cigarette holder, Aivas was displeased with the saliva-soaked paper and tobacco crumbs that were stuck to his lips.

This prompted him to invent a brand of cigarettes that required no cigarette holder. Each cigarette would have its own small cork tip at the end that would allow a person to smoke it without the typical "mess" associated with paper cigarettes. The "filter" was made from crepe paper and did little to block tar and nicotine from escaping the smoke.

Though not popular at the time, filtered cigarettes would become a huge industry by the 1960's, eventually outselling their non-filtered brethren. By that time, the "need" for filters was seen more as a health concern rather than for convenience.

The modern tan, speckled cellulose filters that are attached to most cigarettes are a visual throwback the obsolete cork filters of the '20's and '30's.

"Portugee" Jack's Impossible Ride

They say that he stood over six feet tall, rode a black horse named Dandy, and carried a wooden snuffbox with a carved skull and crossbones on the lid, which he "liberated" from a Sioux Indian chief. His name was John "Jack" Phillips, known to his friends and countrymen as "Portugee Jack."

Though his exploits have faded from public memory over the years, Wyoming folklorists still recall his superhuman feat of endurance that took place through the awful blizzard of 1866-1867.

Portugee Jack was born Manual Felipe Cardoso on April 8, 1832 on the island of Pico, making him a Portuguese citizen by birth. As a teenager, he left the Azore Isle to pan for gold during the California Gold Rush. For the next 15 years, he mined for gold wherever the rumors of big strikes were happening. During this period, Jack traveled all over the land that would one day become the United States of America, a feat that most frontiersman of his day found impressive.

In June of 1866, Colonel Henry B. Carrington was ordered to defend a large group of settlers as they made their way down the Bozeman Trail. Along with his 700 soldiers, he enlisted the help of 300 civilians, mostly miners. Portugee Jack was one of these volunteers.

Along the way, the group was cursed with sporadic Indian attacks that left several pioneer families and soldiers dead. The settlers finally reached their destination three months later and construction of a permanent settlement began immediately.

During the building of the settlement, the group withstood 50 separate Indian attacks within a three month period. Something had to be done about the marauding Natives, and the Cavalry sent Lieutenant Horatio S. Bingham and Infantry Captains William J. Fetterman and James W. Powell to the camp, now called Fort Kearny, in order to mount an offense against the various hostile tribes.

Though Fetterman was an accomplished Civil War veteran, he had no experience fighting Indians, and blamed the repeated Indian attacks against meek military leadership. "Give me 80 men," he boasted, "and I'll run through the entire damn Sioux nation."

One of the 80 men picked for the expedition was Portugee Jack, singled out for his invaluable experience with both the land and the Indian tribes. The militia tried a half dozen times to launch an offense against the Indians, with each attack ending with the Cavalrymen retreating back to camp. Portugee Jack knew that trying to overthrow the Indians was a fool's folly, but the promise of $300 at the end of the campaign kept him from deserting.

Fetterman decided to launch a "massive" attack against the combined forces of several local tribes. Unbeknownst to him, almost 1,000 Indians had banded together to launch a counterattack. Portugee Jack, one of three scouts, rushed back to warn Fetterman of the massive army awaiting them. Fetterman sent Jack, along with Daniel Dixon and Robert Bailey, to the nearest telegraph location, about 200 miles away. The temperature was already sub-zero, but the three men left the group of soldiers, most likely knowing that by the time help arrived, they would all be dead. All told, the Indians lost about 160 men, while all 80 of Fetterman's men were killed.

Caught in a blizzard deep in Sioux territory, Daniel Dixon decided to break loose and make it to a nearby fort, leaving Jack and Bailey alone to complete their mission. Starving and frostbitten, the two men finally reached the telegraph post at Horseshoe Station on Christmas day, 1866. Their ride had ended up being in vain, for the relentless blizzard had destroyed the telegraph lines.

The only other telegraph station was about 40 miles away. Jack ate a hot bowl of soup and quickly donned his gear and headed out towards Fort Laramie. Bailey and the men at the station begged Jack not to go, for "he was as close to death as any man I'd ever seen," according to Bailey.

In two days, a walking corpse of a man stumbled into the Laramie station, where a formal ball was taking place, and collapsed on the floor. Women fainted as the giant man covered in buffalo fur passed out, his skin blue and pulse faint. After regaining consciousness, Jack delivered his message and word was sent out to the Cavalry who arrived nearly a month later, only to find that in addition to the 80 soldiers dead at "Fetterman's Massacre," the Indians also killed or wounded another 160 men, women and children at Fort Kearney.

Jack and the men that rode with him were given their $300 and Jack received the "best horse in Company F of the 2nd Cavalry." He went on to become a mail carrier for the US Postal Service and survived several minor skirmishes with hostile Indians along the way. He was once ambushed by fifteen Sioux. One arrow grazed his head and the other went into his inner thigh, but he managed to kill six of the Indians before the others could retreat. He stated that "without aid of my faithful horse, and good revolver, I would have lost my hair, and the part of my body I feel most anxious about on the prairies."

Jack later married a Cheyenne Indian woman, Hattie Buck, and the couple had nearly a dozen children, one of which was ironically named Paul Revere Phillips. Jack spent the rest of his life as a rancher and hotel operator, passing away November 18, 1933. His wife died in Los Angeles at the age of 94, in 1936. His skull-and-crossbones snuffbox is on permanent display at the University of Wyoming in Laramie.

The Use of Tobacco: An Overview of the History of Medical Research Regarding Tobacco Use From the 15th Century Until Today

By Steven I. Hajdu and
Manjunath S. Vadmal

Editor's Note: We wish to thank the ACS for permission to reprint this study, which is a fairly inclusive overview of the medical community's views towards tobacco over the course of the last 500 years.

There is no written record in reference to tobacco prior to the 15th century. However, it is generally acknowledged that indigenous Americans used tobacco as a medicine and smoked tobacco. In 1492, Christopher Columbus (1451–1506) and his crew, when returning to Europe from the Americas, brought the first tobacco leaves and seeds into Europe. In 1560, Jean Nicot (1530–1600), French diplomat and importer, introduced tobacco in France and Portugal. By the end of the 16th century, tobacco use had became a custom among fashionable people in Europe and tobacco was being exported to India, China, and Japan [1, 2].

Tobacco is an annual plant belonging to the eggplant family. Tobacco was named after Tobago, the island in the West Indies from whence the major part of the tobacco used in Europe was imported. Although the leaves have an acrid taste, tobacco enjoyed widespread medicinal use from the beginning of the 16th century to the end of the 19th century.

According to two privately printed monographs, the beneficial uses of tobacco were almost endless [3, 4]. Finely ground tobacco, snuff, was sniffed as a remedy for colds, headache, and eye problems. Chewing tobacco was sold in the form of loose leaf or plugs to be held in the cheeks. In Asian countries, tobacco was chewed mixed with betel nuts and lime. Chewing tobacco was recommended for toothache, gum diseases, aches in the throat, and mental depression. Decanted liquor of boiled tobacco was used internally to treat indigestion, aches in the belly, and urinary obstruction. Ashes of burned tobacco were mixed with hog grease and applied as an ointment to ulcerated skin, warts, and dermal cancer. Smoking tobacco was claimed to improve body odor and to prevent the plague. Persons of all ages and classes smoked excessively during the great epidemics. Smoking tobacco was believed to calm the nerves and relieve anxiety by purging the brain. Smoke blown into the ear cured earache and when applied to the anus relieved constipation and bloody discharge. Tobacco juice dropped into the ears improved deafness. Tobacco that was made into a syrup with honey was used to treat asthma, chest diseases, cough, and syphilis [3,4].

As time went by, it was recognized that tobacco was not a cure-all. In 1601, an anonymous pamphlet, "Work for Chimney-Sweepers," was distributed in London. The pamphlet described tobacco as a poison and indicated that medicinal use of tobacco or smoking was harmful because it deprived the body of nourishment, dried up men's sperm, and had a stupefying effect, not unlike opium. The pamphlet added that tobacco should be avoided by young people and pregnant women because tobacco weakened the body [5].

In 1604, King James I of England rendered a written warning that smoking was harmful to the eye, nose, brain, and lungs [6]. He placed a heavy duty and a local tax on imported tobacco. Korea and Japan introduced a ban on smoking to prevent fires. China and Turkey prohibited smoking to prevent an inbalance of trade with foreign countries. In 1660, England prohibited the planting of tobacco and placed restrictions on selling imported tobacco. Coalitions of women were formed against tobacco in many countries. They claimed, among other things, that tobacco diminished male virility and they advised women not to marry smokers. For those who were married to a smoker, it was lawful to become divorced [5].

In 1620, Thomas Venner of London warned against smoking [7]. In his book, he wrote that immoderate use of tobacco hurts the brain and the sight, diminishes digestion, and induces trembling of the limbs and the heart. He advised that tobacco should be limited to medicinal use and should not be consumed for pleasure.

In 1761, John Hill (1716–1775), a London surgeon, reported ulcerated cancers of the nose in two men who had used large quantities of snuff for many years [8]. In 1795, Samuel T. Soemmerring (1755–1830), Professor of Anatomy at Mainz, reported an association between pipe smoking and cancer of the lower lip [9]. In 1844, Walter Walshe (1812–1892), a London pathologist, published a book on cancer [10] in which he cited smoking, mechanical irritation, mental affliction, drunkenness, and constitutional predisposition as causes of neoplasia.

In the 1800s, chemists isolated the active ingredient in tobacco and named it nicotine in memory of Jean Nicot, who imported tobacco into Europe in the 1500s. Nicotine is an alkaloid, $C_{10}H_{14}N_2$, that is one of the most potent vegetable poisons. The proportion of nicotine in different varieties of tobacco varies from 2 to 8 percent. Pure nicotine is a colorless oily liquid. It boils at 240°F, it becomes brown and crystallizes on exposure to air, and it dissolves in water, alcohol, and oils [11]. The smallest quantity of nicotine capable of causing death of a person is unknown, but it is probable, that 2 or 3 drops of pure nicotine may be fatal. The poisonous effects of freshly prepared nicotine may be almost as rapid as those of cyanide or hemlock. Death is caused by respiratory arrest. Several cases were reported of accidental, suicidal, or homicidal fatalities by medicinal infusions or enemas of tobacco, or by the ingestion of food and wine contaminated with snuff or chewing tobacco [11].

Medicinal use of tobacco gradually decreased in the 1800s, but was replaced by the habit of smoking for pleasure. Celebrities, for example the Baroness de Dudevant, Frederic Chopin's mistress, who was reportedly the first woman to smoke in public in Paris, gave a helping hand to tobacconists to sell a new product, hand-rolled cigarettes. The chewing of tobacco and pipe smoking continued into the 1900s and cigarette smoking became increasingly popular. In the 1920s, Frederick Hoffman, statistician of the Prudential Company of America, carried out a statistical survey to see if there were any health problems associated with tobacco smoking [12]. He analyzed his cases with consideration of the kind of tobacco used, the method of smoking, the quantity smoked, and the age at which the subject had begun to smoke. He concluded that the increase in cancer of the lung, to a certain extent, was directly traceable to cigarette smoking and he added that older methods of smoking (eg, pipe, cigar) were *more* injurious than the smoking of cigarettes.

In 1941, Alton Ochsner and Michael DeBakey, two American thoracic surgeons, observed that the increase in lung cancer was due to increased production of automobiles and consumption of tobacco [13]. They added that, despite the gravity of pulmonary cancer, due to its early detection and advances in surgical therapy, the prognosis was becoming relatively favorable.

In 1950, a retrospective study in the United States implicated tobacco smoking as a possible etiologic factor in bronchiogenic carcinoma [14]. The authors, Ernest Wynder and Evarts Graham, reported that 94% of 605 men with bronchiogenic carcinoma were cigarette smokers, 4% were pipe smokers, and 2% smoked cigars. The influence of tobacco smoking on the development of adenocarcinoma was much less than on the other histologic types of bronchiogenic carcinoma.

Also in 1950, a preliminary prospective study of a cohort of lung cancer patients in England by Richard Doll and Bradford Hill [15] showed that 100% of the men and 68% of the women were smokers. The authors emphasized that 32% of the female lung cancer patients were nonsmokers.

In 1957, Oscar Auerbach (1905–1997), an American pathologist, and his associates compared tissue sections from the tracheobronchial tree of smokers vs nonsmokers [16]. They found that basal cell hyperplasia, squamous metaplasia, and carcinoma in situ were less frequent in those who never smoked, and that the microscopic changes were progressively more severe in the moderate and heavy smokers

In 1958, Cuyler Hammond and Daniel Horn [17] analyzed the mortality of men in the USA and concluded that the death rate of regular cigarette smokers was 68% higher than that of a comparable group of men who had never smoked [17]. The death rate of those who had smoked only occasionally was not significantly different from the death rate of men who had never smoked. Furthermore, the death rate of men who had given up cigarette smoking for a year or more was lower than that of men who continued smoking.

In 1964, the Surgeon General of the United states, Luther Terry, supported by an Advisory Committee, announced that cigarette smoking is hazardous to health and causally related to lung cancer and cancer of the larynx [18].

Trends in tobacco use in the United States from 1890 to 1990, published by the National Institutes of Health [19], show that before 1930, consumption of smokeless tobacco (ie, snuff and chewing tobacco) was most common, but that cigarette use climbed during and after World War II, so that by 1950, 50% of adults in the United States smoked cigarettes.

Five hundred years of recorded history of the use of tobacco is more informative and educational than many other topics in medical history. It is worth remembering the way that medicinal uses of an herb, tobacco, induced its consumption for pleasure hundreds of years ago. Despite sporadic warnings about the potential harm that tobacco may inflict on its abusers, it took nearly 450 years to apprehend and distinguish the true and falsely claimed consequences of tobacco use.

REFERENCES

1. Mayne RG. *Expository Lexicon.* J Churchill, London, 1860.

2. Motherby G. *Medical Dictionary.* J Johnson, London, 1791.

3. Monardes N. *Hearbes.* Seville, 1571.

4. Wateson G. *Cures of the Diseased.* London, 1598.

5. Mullett CF. *Tobacco as a drug in earlier English medicine.* Ann Med History 1940; 2:110–123.

6. *A Counter Blast to Tobacco.* By "RB," London, 1604.

7. Venner T. *Via Recta.* E Griffin, London, 1620.

8. Hill J. *Cautions Against the Immoderate Use of Snuff.* R Baldwin, London, 1761.

9. Von Soemmering ST. *De Morbis Vasorum.* Varrentrapp u. Wenner, Frankfurti, 1795.

10. Walshe WH. *The Anatomy, Physiology, Pathology, and Treatment of Cancer.* WD Ticknor, Boston, 1844.

11. Witthaus RA, Beckner TC. *Medical Jurisprudence, Forensic Medicine and Toxicology.* W Wood, New York, 1896.

12. Hoffman FL. *Cancer and smoking habits.* In: Cancer (Adair FE, Ed), JB Lippincott, Philadelphia, 1931; pp 50–67.

13. Ochsner A, DeBakey M. *Carcinoma of the lung.* Arch Surg 1941;42:209–258.

14. Wynder EL, Graham EA. *Tobacco smoking as a possible etiologic factor in bronchiogenic carcinoma.* JAMA 1950;143:329–336.

15. Doll R, Bradford Hill A. *Smoking and carcinoma of the lung.* Br Med J 1950;2:739–748.

16. Auerbach O, Brewster G, Forman JB, et al. *Changes in the bronchial epithelium in relation to smoking and cancer of the lung.* NEJM 1957; 256: 97–104.

17. Hammond EC, Horn D. *Smoking and death rates.* JAMA 1958; 166:1159–1172.

18. Anon. *Smoking and Health. Report of the Advisory Committee to the Surgeon General of the Public Health Service.* U.S. Department of Health, Washington, DC, 1964.

19. Anon. *Smokeless Tobacco and Health. National Institutes of Health* Publication 93–3461. Washington, DC, 1993.

STE

NOT ALL SNUS
IS CREATED EQUAL.

SWEDISH SNUS

General®

NORDIC MINT
15 PORTIONS

WARNING: This product can
cause gum disease and

WARNING: This product can cause
gum disease and tooth loss.

The EU ENVI Vote: Crushing Blow For Users of Non-lethal Tobacco Products

By Larry Waters

(This article originally appeared on Snuscentral.org, © Larry Waters 2013)

The EU Committee on the Environment, Public Health and Food Safety (ENVI) July 10th, 2013 vote on the next EU Tobacco Products Directive (TPD) ended in disaster for Reduced Harm advocates.

The fight is not over but the future of Swedish snus and e-cigarettes are now very much in doubt.

The Swedish Exemption on Snus remains. While an exemption for snus from upcoming EU flavoring bans was approved, an exemption on an ingredients ban was voted down thanks to UK MEP Linda McAvan.

Sweden seemed to believe it had support from McAvan to get an ingredients exemption which would continue to allow baking soda (fondly known as E500) to be used in Swedish snus.

Why should snusers care about a little baking soda in their snus? Without E500, one cannot extract nicotine from snus.

Maria Larsson's poor strategy of trading the Swedish snus ban for flavoring protection, a weak and myopic negotiating point to begin with, has driven Swedish snus to the very edge of disaster.

With an ingredients ban that removes substances that promote nicotine uptake (E500 and the like, in the case of snus), McAvan has set up a possible backdoor ban of snus in Sweden. What is snus without bio-available nicotine? We're not just talking Strong and Extra Strong snus; all snus brands would have less available nicotine than a half a piece of 2mg nicotine gum.

The ENVI vote was very close; 34-34 with MEP McAvan driving the stake into the heart of the Swedish snus ingredients ban for now.

I predict this won't stop Minister Larsson from issuing press releases tomorrow loudly proclaiming "Fear not; our snus has been saved; Sweden can regulate flavorings without EU interference."

Missing from these press releases will be any mention of the ban on ingredients that facilitate nicotine uptake. Without these ingredients, Swedes will have tobacco brimming with any flavor they like under their lip but have no ability to access the nicotine!

E-Cigarettes now Regulated as Pharmaceutical Products; Menthol Banned

"What, me crazy?" McAvan does her best Alfred E. Neuman impression.

In another stunning decision, ENVI voted to regulate e-Cigarettes in the EU as Medicinal Products while combustible cigarettes remain regulated as Consumer Products.

While I agree e-cigarettes have not been around long enough to know the long-term effects of inhaling concentrated propylene glycol, we all know the deadly long-term effects of inhaling cigarette smoke containing tar and 5,000 to 10,000 known toxins, carcinogens, and substances science hasn't been able to quite identify yet.

Menthol cigarettes will be banned but not because menthol is a health hazard. The Press has ridiculed Former German chancellor Helmut Schmidt for panic-buying 38,000 menthol cigarettes before any menthol ban can be instituted. I am not one of those making jokes.

Like Schmidt, I am a nicotine addict. I lived through the pre-PACT Act snus hoarding in 2009. I bought an extra freezer just to hold my snus reserves. If we get down to the wire on an E500 ban in Sweden, I will be taking out a second mortgage to import and cold-store as much Swedish Snus as I can get my hands on.

If I haven't died of old age by the time my snus runs out, I'll turn to vaping (if that is still legal in the USA). As a final option, I can always go back to smoking cigarettes, assuming FDA has left any meaningful levels of nicotine in them. It won't be for long; I'm sure returning to combustible cigarettes will kill me much sooner than later. Good thing I was never a menthol smoker.

What's Next for Swedish Snus and E-cigarettes in the new EU Evil Empire?

The next round is when the proposed TPD goes to Plenary in September/October. There will be quite a fight there because MEP Linda McAvan has basically ignored a large voice in Parliament, and not just on the Snus/E-cigarette issues.

After today's ENVI vote, if Sweden is still counting on McAvan to save snus, I fear for snus.

Fortunately, snus and Sweden have a great friend and champion in Swedish MEP Christofer Fjellner. Mr. Fjellner also runs a very popular quasi-legal Swedish snus store out of his office in Brussels. Rumors that Moe Unz is a silent partner in this endeavor are completely false. Anyone who knows Moe knows he can't keep a secret after three drinks.

Fjellner: The Snus Savior?

After today's ENVI session,, Mr. Fjellner rushed to his blog and posted an excellent article entitled After vote – Recap of the vote on the Tobacco Products Directive. It is well worth reading.

Meanwhile, if you're a citizen of the UK, I would strongly suggest addressing MEP McAvan as to the error of her ways when it comes to snus, the Swedish snus ban, and all Reduced Harm products. She needs to place the public health above her own personal prejudices and political agenda.

Brussels should be mindful of another point as the TPD process approaches its conclusion.

Since joining the EU, Sweden has consistently shown that as long as modern snus in Sweden for Swedes is maintained, they will surrender the principle of free and open trade even though it is against their own best interests. Stockholm seems very timid when it comes to international relationships and are not the best negotiators.

If the ingredients ban does end up in the final TPD effectively ending Swedish snus, that timidity will disappear in a flash. Sweden will leave the EU by demand of the Swedish people. The example Sweden's exit sets will inspire others increasing unhappy with the Brussels Autocracy such as the UK to follow suit. Say goodbye to your dreams of a European Empire (you know who you are).

Swedish Snus über alles!

Larry Waters

ABRAXAS

PREMIUM BATCH ENGLISH SNUFF

ab actu ab posse valet illatio

Warning: This product is not a safe alternative to cigarettes.

Hey Kids! Free Puke!

Help Sell THE SNUFF TAKER'S EPHEMERIS to all of your friends, enemies, family, teachers and clergymen! They'll love our articles and beg to buy more. Why, you could make dozens of dollars if you just work 20 hours a day until you hit puberty and realize how stupid this whole thing was!

IMITATION VOMIT

Amazingly realistic PUKE! Looks like someone was SICK, SICK, SICK! almost turns your stomach to use as joke, it's so realistic. Made of plastic. The "gloppiest" look. Place by baby, dog, dinner table or pretend you've been sick. Most revolting, dirtiest trick we've seen. (Created a riot when we tested it!)

No. 2636. Price Postpaid. . . . . **50¢**

Here's How It Works:

You send us 398.00 and we'll send you a box of 40 magazines. Somehow you get other people to buy each copy for more than you paid for it. Then you send us a check or money order for 398.00 and we'll send you the FREE VOMIT (a .50 value). That's right- you get to KEEP ABOUT 2.00 (total may vary depending on how successful you are) and a piece of fake vomit (a 50 Cent Value!) Absolutely FREE! (Minus the upfront $398 cost of the magazines. NON- REFUNDABLE.)

So when your parents ask you why you've been up for days, shaking badly and walking into walls, just show them that it's because YOU want to be a SELF-MADE man by selling the STE like a REAL businessman. Instead of playing with your friends, you'll be out every day trying to turn an impossible profit. No tricks, no gimmicks, just good old-fashioned door to door rejection.

☐ I'm a stupid kid who just stole 400 bucks out of my mom's purse and I can barely read or write, much less do math. Please send me a stack of magazines I'll never end up selling.

☐ I'm not an idiot. I want to subscribe to your magazine and take advantage of all the good deals like quantity discounts and free shipping. I'm going to www.STEphemeris.com to find the subscription package that suits me best.

Snus King:

Ljunglöf's *Ettan* And The History Of Swedish Snus

An Ephemeris Exclusive

Original text by the Swedish Tobacco Museum

CHAPTER EIGHT:
STATE MONOPOLY

THE SNUS KING ABDICATES

Knut Ljunglöf, even amid the scandals and personal matters that marred his family, continued to be the most successful snuff manufacturer in all of Europe. In fact, he was the richest man in Sweden. Only the mighty Lorillard factory in the United States produced more snuff than Ljunglöf; *Ettan* came in a close second, and was continuing to grow every day, though a dark cloud loomed on the horizon.

Just when the new factory in Badstugatan was built, World War 1 broke out and Sweden was thrown into disarray. Talks of a state Tobacco Monopoly had been bandied about for years, but no one, least of all Knut, took the threat seriously.

But the Swedish government saw things differently. Soldiers and farmers were receiving a pension from the government, and the World War made it impossible for the treasury to pay these pensions. It was decided that the Swedish government would take over the tobacco industry, with the profits going out to pay the pensions owed.

This was the final blow for Knut. For the last few years, he had been running the Ettan company side by side with his son Robert, teaching him the ropes. But now that the government swooped in to take most of his money and commandeer his business holdings, he simply gave up the ghost. He retired fully and let Robert Ljunglöf take over the affairs of the snus factories, which were now wholly owned by the state. It was a crushing end for the man who worked all of his life to end up with nothing to show for it.

By 1915, Sweden had taken over all of the tobacco production within the country. Most snus makers were allowed to continue running their factories, and were paid a fair sum for their holdings.

Above: The Ljunglöf Factory as it looked circa 1915.

One famous anecdote concerns the transition of the Ettan factories from the Ljunglöf family over to the Tobacco Monopoly. As the State Appraiser took inventory of everything in the Ettan factory, he was astonished by the overwhelming supply of Grade A Virginia tobacco, a rarity in Sweden. The Appraiser turned to Robert, astonished. "You have more Virginia tobacco in this one factory than exists in all of Sweden!"

Young Robert, proud of his family's legacy, answered nonchalantly. "Of course we use only the finest tobacco, or it wouldn't be called *Ettan*!"

love and idol. As he lay on his deathbed, Knut gathered decades worth of personal correspondence, business receipts, and top secret snus recipes and set fire to them all. Sick with pneumonia, the embittered old man wanted his former empire to die with him.

But not all of the Ljinglöf family mementos went into the fireplace. After Knut's death, many such documents were recovered and used as the basis for the remarkable biography of the Ljunglöf dynasty, *En gammal Stockholmsfirmas historia* by Ludwig Lubbe Nördstrom. It was written in 1930 at the behest of Robert.

THE BITTER END

Robert received more free capital after the sale of the Tobacco factories than his father or grandfather could have ever dreamed of. He turned the Ettan empire over to the Monopoly with no strings attached save for one: that the money reaped by the country from his company went directly to the farmers pensions that had been the impetus for forming the Monopoly in the first place. When Robert found out that some farmers had been removed from their farms, he sold off the family's fleet of luxury cars and turned the money over to the farmers so that they could get their old farms back.

Robert proved to be as astute a businessman as his father and grandfather. Inspired by his friend Ivar Krueger, he invested heavily in the pharmaceutical and chemical industries in addition to buying up several insurance companies. The "old" snus factory at Sveavägen 44 was demolished and Robert built an office complex for his insurance company *Thule*, later renamed *Skandia*.

Papa Knut passed away and Robert moved the family to their estate at Beateberg, which was often visited by singer Jenny Lind, Knut's early

Below: The bust of King Knut, which was made shortly before his death and printed along with his obituary in all of Sweden's newspapers.

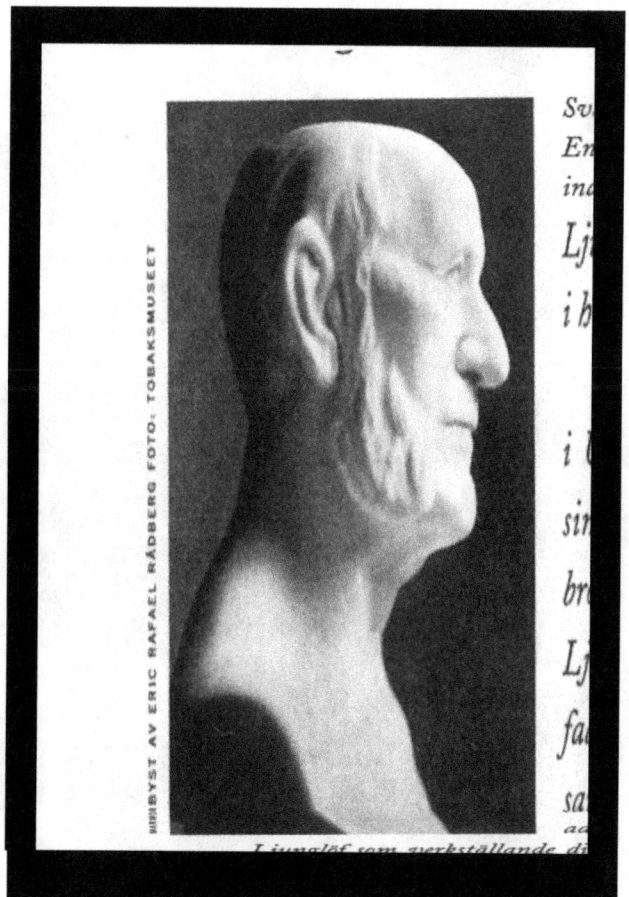

MINIBYST AV ERIC RAFAEL RÅDBERG FOTO: TOBAKSMUSEET

Epilog

ETTAN: THE BASTARD CHILD

The King Majesty's Bill Number 254, passed July 20th, 1914, nationalized the distribution of Ettan, an honor that was not bestowed upon the other 100 odd factories that the Monopoly absorbed. Production of Ettan continued in the 1920s, then moved to Tobacco Monopoly headquarters in Rosenlundsgatan in Stockholm, then finally ended up at Hultmans Islet adjacent the Gota river in Göteborg, where the country's only remaining snus factory run by Swedish Match resides today **[Note: this is no longer the case, Swedish Match has expanded significantly since this book was originally written]**.

The improved, streamlined Ettan package. This was the new container that Ettan was sold in after the State Tobacco Monopoly took over production.

Ettan (and other brands) were sold in a wide variety of packages, ranging from kegs, karduser (see below), tin cans, and various wooden containers of all shapes and sizes. However, the future lied in cardboard (introduced in the ovular container in 1907) which gradually made all other packaging obsolete.

The cardboard packaging kept the snus fresher for a longer duration and the convenient size and shape meant that the home-made birch snuff boxes that practically every man carried at the time were no longer needed. Most of these birch snuff boxes were given to children as a plaything. A popular sight of the day was a child playing with a snuffbox with two thin pieces of metal wire stuck through both sides of the box, resembling the axles of an automobile. Crude wooden or cardboard wheels were attached to the "axles," and the child now had a toy car to play with, complete with a removable, wooden convertible top!

The limited run of Kardus Editions of Swedish Match lös snus series 2012. Karduser packages were made of waxed paper that was then wrapped with blue, inner-foiled paper that was topped of with a paper brand banner looped around the width of the box. These versions of the classic Swedish trademarks are hand-made in extremely limited quantities at the Swedish Tobacco Museum in Stockholm using the same exact ingredients and production methods that date to the early 1800s.

But not all of the non-cardboard packages disappeared. Up until 1990, retailers and customers could still order bulk, wooden kegs of Ettan for nostalgic or practical reasons. Also available were 15 pound waxed cardboard containers.

After the Tobacco Monopoly took over the production of Ettan, the consumers didn't seem to mind. After all, this was still Ljuglöf's Ettan. It was the same snus, just with a different company producing it. The original minimalist recipe (salt, potash, tobacco and water) had not changed since the days of J. F. Ljunglöf, and much to Swedish Match's credit, this same recipe is still used today. Rumors that Ettan was being flavored artificially to achieve the chocolaty flavor it was world-renowned for were just that- rumors. The unique flavor is still achieved by blending the 20 or so correct types of tobacco that give Ettan its nutty, almost coffee-like flavor. The only flavoring ingredient that has ever been used in Ettan is plain, everyday table salt. The moisture content increased under Knut's supervision in order to accommodate the nasal snuffers who were then using snus orally. When left to dry out, a

modern can of Ettan is just as enjoyable as a nasal snuff as it is an oral snus.

In 1967, the State Tobacco Monopoly was dissolved and the snus industry was privatized into the STA (Swedish Tobacco Authority, forerunner of today's Swedish Match.) Snus production was now open to everyone who wanted to make it. This caused an increase in new snus brands, with several smaller companies opening up seemingly overnight. Most of them disappeared as quickly as they appeared, unable to compete with the mighty Juggernaut that was the STA.

But one such brand threatened to take away some of Ettan's marketshare. At that time, Ettan was still the best-selling snus brand worldwide. (Today it is number two behind General.) In 1967, a new snus was hitting store shelves with the name **Ljunglöf's Original Ettan.** The snus was being manufactured by J.F. Ljunglöf's great grandson, Captain Knut Jacob Ljunglöf. Captain Knut was the son of the offspring of Knut Sr.'s first marriage. Whether this was an attempt to bring back some of the pride associated with his family's name, or just a cheap way to cash in on the success of Ettan is unsure. But the STA quickly sued, and the Swedish court's ruled that Captain Knut could sell his version of Ettan by mail order only, so as not to confuse the consumer at the retail level. Captain Knut's "Original Ettan" is still being manufactured under license to this day by several small, regional snus makers who sometimes sell the brand under different names so as not to provoke the ire of Swedish Match. If you are ever lucky(?) enough to find one of these retailers, "Original Ettan" is usually sold with the name "Kaptain" or "No. 1" somewhere in the title.

Svenska Tobaks AB proved that although blood may be thicker than water, in the case of Ettan, there can be only one.

The STE would like to thank the following companies and individuals who made this translation possible: Fredrik Olsson, Swedish Match AB and NA, the Swedish Tobacco Museum, the original authors, and the readers who asked us to do it in the first place.

STE

How Many Lives?

By Dr. Lars-Erik Rutqvist

(Note: this article originally appeared in Aftenposten, *August 16, 2013.)*

Tom K. Grimsrud of the Cancer Registry knows that Smokeless Tobacco is 90 percent less harmful than cigarettes. Yet he chose, in *Aftenposten* two days ago, to continue to spread disinformation about the link between tobacco and adverse health effects. A debate about the health effects of "pleasure products" is important, but only if it is based on facts and not scare tactics.

In the article in *Aftenposten*, Grimsrud argues that it is a bad idea to replace cigarettes with snuff and snus, which increases the risk of cancer. The Royal College of Physicians have concluded that smokeless tobacco is at least 90 percent less harmful than cigarettes. **[Note: The Ephemeris still stands by the other, more thoroughly researched studies that show smokeless tobacco to be at least 98% safer than cigarette smoking.]** It is now over 10 years since the EU, from a scientific standpoint, removed cancer warning on snuff tins. The fact is that if everyone who smoked converted to snuff it would have had major positive health effects.

Norwegian smokers' lives could be spared had they been advised of the health difference between snus and cigarettes. This has happened in Sweden, and is about to happen in Norway. Smokeless tobacco is still tobacco, but it has few or none of the negative health effects of cigarettes. On the contrary, snuff is the most widely used (and clinically proven) most effective means to stop smoking. Everyone knows someone who has quit smoking by using snus or snuff. A committee of experts who work on behalf of the EU Health Authority in 2008 concluded that the Swedish public health has improved because many smokers have quit using smokeless tobacco.

Grimsrud argues that the WHO Cancer Research (IARC) has concluded that smokeless tobacco causes cancer. This is a gross oversimplification. IARC has concluded that it is smokeless tobacco as a whole that must be regarded as carcinogenic. This category includes many different products, from products that are almost as harmful as cigarettes on one end of the scale to snuff and snus on the other end. The IARC report from 2009 is based primarily on research on African and Indian products which have health effects that look more like cigarettes than smokeless tobacco.

Third page over: will European and American convenience stores look like this one day? One can only hope.

Q: What's New From
★★★
SWEDISH MATCH ?

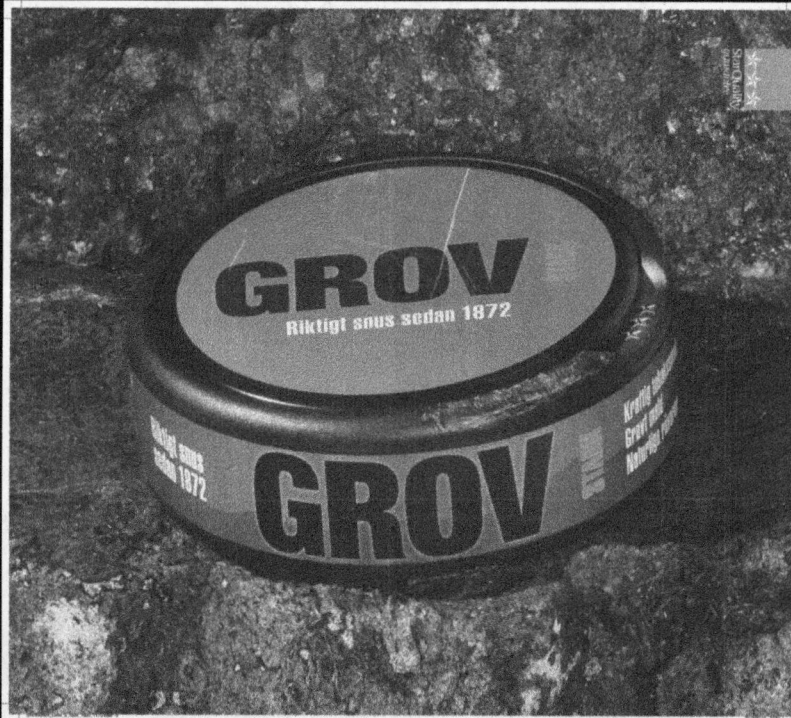

A: Everything.

New flavors. Expanded Distribution. Improved pouch material. New can designs. All at the same reasonable price you've come to expect from the world's greatest snus maker.

Available now from Snuscentral.Com and other fine tobacconists worldwide.

Grimsrud did not mention is that WHO has compared the health effects of smokeless tobacco with nicotine medicines. Swedish snus produced by the industry standard GothiaTek have lower levels of unwanted items (nitrosamines and bone pyrene) than the limits WHO recommends for smokeless tobacco.

On one point, Grimsrud is absolutely right. Pregnant and breastfeeding women should not use anything containing nicotine, whether it be smokeless tobacco or pharmaceutical nicotine replacement drugs.

In the years that I was head of cancer registry in Stockholm (part of the Swedish Cancer Registry) our biggest goal was to to prevent cancer and thus contribute to a better public health. It does not seem like Grimsrud shares that view. He avoids discussing the potential of snuff to prevent both cancer and cardiovascular disease among smokers.

We must have an active debate about the health effects of products Norwegians use. The debate should be based on facts, which are absent from Grimstad's statements in *Aftenposten.*

Dr. Lars Erik Rutqvist is one of Sweden's premiere cancer specialists and is world renowned for his research into smokeless tobacco.

ElishaC Photography
WWW.ELISHAC.WEBS.COM
ELISHACPHOTOGRAPHY@GMAIL.COM

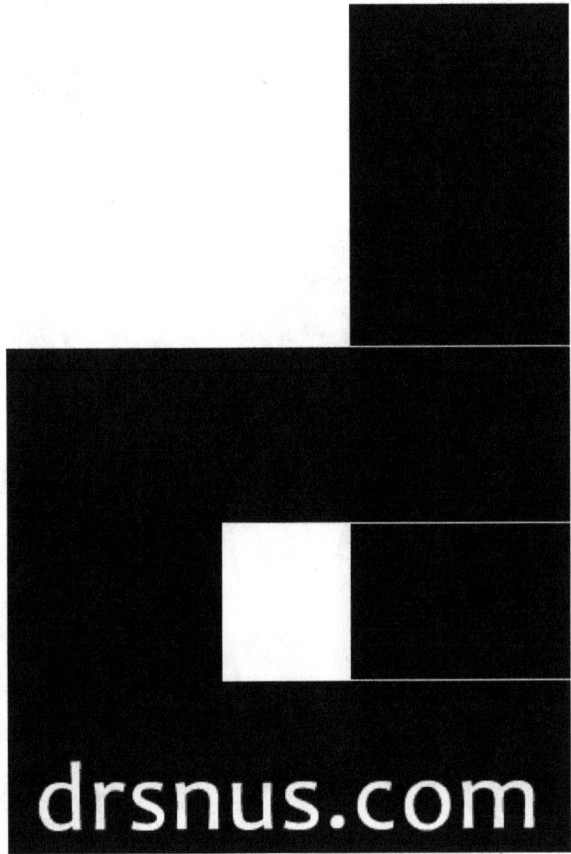
drsnus.com

Hey Kids! Free Puke!

Help Sell THE SNUFF TAKER'S EPHEMERIS to all of your friends, enemies, family, teachers and clergymen! They'll love our articles and beg to buy more. Why, you could make dozens of dollars if you just work 20 hours a day until you hit puberty and realize how stupid this whole thing was!

IMITATION VOMIT

Amazingly realistic PUKE! Looks like someone was SICK, SICK, SICK! almost turns your stomach to use as joke, it's so realistic. Made of plastic. The "gloppiest" look. Place by baby, dog, dinner table or pretend you've been sick. Most revolting, dirtiest trick we've seen. (Created a riot when we tested it!)

No. 2636. Price Postpaid. . . . . **50¢**

Here's How It Works:

You send us 398.00 and we'll send you a box of 40 magazines. Somehow you get other people to buy each copy for more than you paid for it. Then you send us a check or money order for 398.00 and we'll send you the FREE VOMIT (a .50 value). That's right- you get to KEEP ABOUT 2.00 (total may vary depending on how successful you are) and a piece of fake vomit (a 50 Cent Value!) Absolutely FREE! (Minus the upfront $398 cost of the magazines. NON- REFUNDABLE.)

So when your parents ask you why you've been up for days, shaking badly and walking into walls, just show them that it's because YOU want to be a SELF-MADE man by selling the STE like a REAL businessman. Instead of playing with your friends, you'll be out every day trying to turn an impossible profit. No tricks, no gimmicks, just good old-fashioned door to door rejection.

☐ I'm a stupid kid who just stole 400 bucks out of my mom's purse and I can barely read or write, much less do math. Please send me a stack of magazines I'll never end up selling.

☐ I'm not an idiot. I want to subscribe to your magazine and take advantage of all the good deals like quantity discounts and free shipping. I'm going to www.**STEphemeris**.com to find the subscription package that suits me best.

By
Simon
Handelsman

The Snuff Box

MULL SNUFF BOXES

The practical mind of humankind is always looking for a solution to a problem. Imagine the delight of the thrifty Scot in figuring out that the tip of a horn could be hollowed out to make a suitable snuff box. Goat, rams and cattle horns were all used. Then, some artisan solved the problem of the tip wearing holes in frugal pockets by flattening the tip of the horn and curling it backward. Eventually silver mountings, hinges, cork stoppers and an extra twist to the tail were added to create the snuff mull: a practical container for snuff used primarily in Scotland.

The typical mull is distinguished by being made of horn, having a hinged top with a silver hinge, band mountings and a spiral tip. The lids of the three mulls in the previous page are made of horn and illustrate the variety of decoration found.

The mull on the left has a simple round plate for the owner's initials mounted on a nicely grained piece of horn. The lid is framed in a pretty scalloped rim. The hinge is constructed of three simple knuckles attached to the band. The quality of the silver appears lower grade and is unmarked as is the case in many silver mounted snuff boxes.

The mull in the center has a detailed cut silver thistle and leaves surmounted by a fan shaped escutcheon for the owners monogram. The plant is engraved with cross hatching on the flower and veins on the leaves. It has a finely made five knuckle decorative hinge attached to the silver rim and the lid. It is monogrammed *EMJ* on both the escutcheon and the band.

The mull on the right has a silver initialed thumb piece that protects the edge of the lid and a hand cut silver thistle with leaves that has been fully engraved. The five knuckle hinge is mounted to a rim that has been silver plated. This is often done for strength rather than cost. The rim is dated "Dec.25/81". This is most likely 1881 rather than 1781 based upon the overall quality. It does demonstrate that mulls were popular gift throughout the 19th century.

The lid of the mulls sits on the top of the horn with an inner bung that fits tightly into the opening holding the lid firmly closed and keeping the snuff fresh. Normally this bung is made from cork, but leather and wood are encountered. Replacement of this closure was common to keep the mull workable and does not affect value.

The value of a mull is based upon its outward appearance. On the left, the plug or bung is cork covered with soft leather for a secure fit. The plug in the center is a replacement cork. The plug on the right shows remnants of the lead, which was thought to keep the snuff fresh, over the cork.

These three better mulls are all mounted with semi-precious stones on silver lids. The silver rim bands are fancier with turnings, ridges, and scalloping. Two of the lids are domed. The horns themselves have more interesting natural markings. The overall quality is a step above the mulls shown in the earlier group.

BELOW: The mull on the left has an orange agate cabochon mounted in the top of a silver dome shaped lid fitted with a scalloped thumb piece at the front.

There is a five knuckle hinge at the rear that echoes the placement of the thumb piece between the ridges to give the mull a nice visual balance. There is no plug because the top fits tightly onto the lower rim. The cover is engraved to signify a gift: "W.R. to G.L.B"

The center mull has a lavender gray variegated stone mounted in a scalloped bezel surrounded by a simple vine style engraving. There is a five knuckle hinge and a small swell at the front of the rim as a thumb piece. The inside of the top has been gold gilded to help prevent corrosion. The top fits tightly with out any plug onto the silver rim which has been embellished with a wavy bottom edge.

The mull on the right has a faceted grey smoky clear stone mounted into a silver dome lid. The lid has been constructed so that the bottom of the stone is enclosed by a gilded hemisphere that projects downward from the inside of the lid. The purpose of the dome is to provide a shiny surface beneath the stone to reflect the light back up through the clear stone giving it more brilliance and color as well as keep the snuff from dirtying the stone. This mull has a lid that snugly fits over the rim to keep the snuff safely within and the air from ruining the snuff. It has a one inch plaque on the front with a 12 word friendship sentiment and is dated 1832.

Snuff mulls are still made today. They are suitable as a container for modern snuffing. Antique models are available on eBay for around $250.

Left:
Ornate Scottish "Full Head" Snuff Mulls were given away as expensive gifts to people of great import. Whole heads of Sheep, Ram and Goat were converted into expensive, exquisite snuff mulls.

Simon Handelsman is one of the world's first and foremost authorities on antique snuffboxes. Visit his site, **www.snuffbox.com** *for rare items and free appraisals.*

A JACK TOOK THE QUEEN'S ACE

AND HER KING'S FACE WAS RED

THE DIAMONDS LAUGHED WHILE
THE CLUBS CRIED

FOR ALL THE HEARTS WERE DEAD

THE KNOWING MASSES GATHERED

BUT STILL ATE WHAT THEY WERE
FED

THEN ALL FELL SILENT AND STOOD
ASIDE

WHEN THEY SAW THAT THE JOKER
LED

Jeff Horn

livelikedragons@gmail.com

liloe's hookah lounge

3069 Cumberland Road Suite 103
Fayetteville, NC
(910) 429 - 4046
www.liloeshookahlounge.com

Parting Shot:

Tobacco is a dirty weed. I like it.
It satisfies no normal need. I like it.
It makes you thin, it makes you lean,
It takes the hair right off your bean
It's the worst darn stuff I've ever seen.
I like it.

~Graham Lee Hemminger, *Tobacco*

STE®

© 2013 Lucien Publishing
Fayetteville, NC

Member: Independent Publisher's Trade Guild of North Carolina
"Providing Readers With Books That Matter"